BUILDING A MILLION DOLLAR DOLLAR SIDE *Hustle*

JULIANA RICHARDS

A POST HILL PRESS BOOK

ISBN: 978-1-68261-621-5
ISBN (eBook): 978-1-68261-622-2

Building A Million Dollar Side Hustle
© 2018 by Juliana Richards
All Rights Reserved

Cover art by San Darshak

Post Hill Press, LLC
New York • Nashville
posthillpress.com

Published in the United States of America

*I would like to dedicate this book to
my father Richard Ibe Unigwe. His strong words of
encouragement, his work ethic and ambition have
everything to do with the woman I am today.*

CONTENTS

CHAPTER 1

MY FATHER, MY MOTHER, MY NIGERIA

I grew up in Lagos, the most populous city in Nigeria. A vibrant melting pot and bustling commercial capital, Lagos is where people from other parts of the country come to pursue their dreams. When I was a child, it was also a city gripped by political upheaval and military coups as the country began a long transition from a military dictatorship to a true democracy. Some of my earliest memories are of people rioting in the streets, of hiding under the bed and hearing gunshots in the distance, and being told to run at school because soldiers were coming. Fear was a constant companion because there was so much instability.

Although in many ways my childhood was not so different from the typical American experience, the confusion and unrest of my Nigeria was echoed in my home life. I grew up in a working class family with a stay-at-home mother who was a strong matriarch and a loving father who worked six days a week for a French construction company to provide his children with a better life than the one he had. But there was one major difference: my father had two wives and split his time between two homes and two families. The practice was officially banned in Lagos State in 2010, but when I was a child it was permitted under civil law in Nigeria.

Even though my mother was the first wife and bore six of my father's nine children, including the oldest and youngest, my father lived with the second wife. My mother never spoke about the second wife, and they never uttered a single word to one another. The only time I ever saw them together was when my father died. Yet because of this arrangement, I grew up with a mother who never felt valued in her marriage.

For good or bad, we are all shaped by our pasts. Our childhood environment, the people who raise us, these are things we cannot choose for ourselves. What we can choose is *how* those things shape us as we pursue the path to our destiny. My father, my mother, my Nigeria were instrumental in shaping me into a woman of poise. I chose to turn to myself to find an inner strength, to believe in myself because so much around me was in turmoil. I became resilient because things were always in flux.

I may not have known it then, but this self-reliance and resilience would later become instrumental as I went from being a penniless immigrant to creating a successful global brand.

My Father: Character and Confidence

I can still remember the moment I became aware for the first time that my father had another family. I don't remember exactly how old I was: old enough to begin to understand that the children who would come to our house to play all the time were something more than cousins or family friends, but too young to understand our complicated family dynamic. One day, as these children were leaving our house, I remember asking my mother in Pidgin English, "Where dem dey go?" When she explained to me that they were going home, I asked, "Why is my dad going with them?" Her response was the last thing I expected to hear: "Because they are your brothers and sister." I remember feeling utterly heartbroken and abandoned. I loved my father, and I didn't want to share him with anyone, much less another family. Over time, it became normalized in my head, but it never felt right in my heart.

Despite the tension between my parents and my own early feelings of abandonment, my father was devoted to all of his children and was a strong, steady influence in my life. Every morning he would come to our house, eat breakfast, and take me and my brothers and sisters to school. After work at the end of the day, he would return home and eat dinner with us before going to his other family's home. He followed this routine every single day of our lives. I lived with my mother and five siblings, while my three half siblings lived with their mother less than half a mile away. We all lived in the same neighborhood of Lagos Island and went to the same school. Whatever my father bought for one household he bought for the other; everything he did, he did double.

My father didn't discriminate between the boys and girls. In fact, in many ways, his daughters had special status in his homes and his heart. If my brothers wanted anything, they knew the best way to get it from our father was to go through us girls. This was not typical parenting in the Igbo Tribe of Nigeria, where traditionally boys have more say so than girls.

He encouraged us to ask questions and to be curious about the world around us. He made me feel that my opinion mattered. He always spoke to us about strength of character, always prepared us for when he wouldn't be here anymore to protect us. We were Daddy's girls, and he hated us being in the kitchen. I remember my mother would always complain, "Who's going to marry these girls if they can't cook, the president's son?"

One of the most important lessons our father taught us was about the importance of education. He instilled in all of us a passion for learning and the understanding that knowledge would be our most powerful tool for success. He wanted us to have the life he never had and was determined to give us the best education he could afford. He sent all of us to Aunty Ayo's Preparatory School (now called Aunty Ayo's International School), a private school in Ikoyi—a former conclave of British expats during colonial rule that to this day is one of the most affluent neighborhoods in all of Africa.

Some of my happiest childhood memories are of our daily car rides with my father to school. He purposely chose the opportunity to have one-on-one time with all of his children since my half-siblings and I went to the same school. Every day we'd pile into his car, the little ones on the older ones' laps, and as we drove through the million-dollar mansions and opulent estates of Ikoyi, he would tell us the story of how he had worked as a maid for a British family when he was a young boy to help provide for his family, what it was like living under colonial rule, of the turmoil he endured during the Biafran tribal war, how he took job after job and worked his way up the ladder to become the successful man he was then. In addition to being the sole breadwinner for his two wives and nine children, my father also supported an extended family that included his own brothers. He would talk about what he had done in his life so that he did not need to depend on anyone for financial support. He shared with us each step he took to better his financial status, which eventually landed him a corporate position. His history became so familiar to us that we could recite it all by heart. He would talk about the past, the present, and what he wanted for us in the future. He had an unshakable view of the world, and there was a constant theme that ran through all his stories: financial independence.

Listening to his stories was an extraordinary opportunity to learn about responsibility and work ethic. It was a gift to have my dad speak about life with me every single day. I heard his firsthand account of colonial times and his striving to stand out and succeed. And he truly was a success. He was able to send his children to private schools and give them the kind of good life that he never envisioned for himself. He was proud of his position and wanted even more for us. His message was simple: *Work harder than everyone else.* I still remember these words: *"Do you want to be like me or do you want to be better than me? When others are sleeping, you need to get up and work."*

I realize now that he was building confidence and letting us know that even if something seemed difficult or impossible, you could do it if you really wanted to succeed. Because of the confidence my father instilled in me, when I came to the U.S. by myself at the age of eighteen with no family and no financial safety net, I simply thought, "Of course I can conquer this big old American dream." I truly believed, sometimes naively, that I could overcome whatever was in my path.

However, while my father was a powerful influence in my life, he was also a source of deep sadness for my mother. He was a great father, but unfortunately, he was a horrible husband.

My Mother: Serial Entrepreneur and Side Hustler

My mother was born in Ogwashi Ukwu, a city in Delta State. Her father was educated and made his living reading and writing letters for people. He had very strong views about a woman's place in the home, but my grandmother was fiercely independent and the marriage was so oppressive that she ran away when my mother was two and never came back. When she left, my grandfather filed for divorce. He took full advantage of the court and his status, and she was left with nothing, not even her children.

Even though my grandmother was left alone and penniless, she had won her freedom, and for her generation it was almost unheard of for a woman to be independent. She settled in Benin City, the capital of Edo State in southern Nigeria, where she opened a beer parlor. It was probably little more than a wooden frame kiosk with a tarp canopy by the side of the road where she sold beer and snacks to passersby, but it was enough for her to make a new life for herself. Over the years, she tried repeatedly to sneak her children out of my grandfather's house, and when my mother was eight or nine, she finally succeeded.

At eighteen my mother moved to Lagos, where she met my father at church. He was nine years older and already established. He was so sure of himself and would always tell her, "I'm going to marry you one day." So my mother became a housewife and a church lady. She had come to religion almost as an act of rebellion against her father. He did not believe in what he used to call an "imported Christian deity." He believed strongly in his traditional ways of worship and wanted to shield my mother from buying into what he considered "Western religious propaganda." When she was a little girl, he would tell her that there was no Christian God, but she would look up into the sky and think there had to be *something*.

Growing up, religion and the church were a huge part of my life. We attended a strict Christian church where we were not allowed to wear jewelry or pants and were expected to cover our hair and wear long sleeves. We probably would have lived at that church full-time if my father wasn't always there to remind my mother that we were kids who needed to have an outside life. Despite his intervention, our home was essentially a matriarchy because my father wasn't there all of the time. My mother ruled, and that meant growing up in a strict religious environment.

As I got older, I began to understand that one of the reasons my mother was engulfed by her religion was because she wasn't fulfilled by her life as a stay-at-home wife and mother. While our parents loved us, my mother did not feel loved by her husband. Like my grandfather, my father also wanted a woman who was only a housewife and stay-at-home mother. He absolutely did not want his wife working outside the home. But my mother, like her mother before her, had the irrepressible spirit of an entrepreneur. She loved to buy and sell things and always had little businesses going on the side. At various points during my childhood, she sold soap, home-baked bread, body lotions, purified water, ice cream, and popsicles. She was always willing to try something new. She didn't have to be an expert. Her attitude was always, "I can teach myself." There was no mind block that kept her from approaching a new challenge with confidence. Growing up around this kind of entrepreneurial spirit instilled me with the belief that there wasn't any type business I couldn't excel at if I put my mind to it.

Sadly, she never got her husband's support in any of her entrepreneurial endeavors. My father would inevitably convince her to shut down whatever business she was running, especially since most of her endeavors were food-related. He wasn't comfortable with her working because he felt that it was demeaning to his financial status to have a wife who earned money by selling food. However, as soon as he would have her shut down one business, she would already be casting her mind to her next venture because she needed to have something of her own. While she lacked for nothing in terms of material goods, she had no financial independence. In fact, if my mother needed anything for the household, she would have to go to us to get it from my dad.

Watching the dynamic between my parents shaped me into the wife, mother, and businesswoman I am today.

My Nigeria: Conflict and Cartoons

I never saw anyone get killed when I was growing up, but I remember hearing the gunfire. I remember being told the soldiers were coming and having to run to safety. I remember not going to school for days because it wasn't safe to leave the house. There was always fear, an anticipation that something bad would happen. I became extremely cautious. When you grow up in a country consumed by unrest, you learn how to run and hide. You learn how to be quick because you have heard stories about the ones who were hit by a stray bullet because they weren't fast enough. You learn that if you see people running, you start running too.

But my Nigeria was also a childhood of normal things, a childhood that probably looked a lot like that of my American counterparts. Despite what was going on in the country politically, I watched cartoons and movies and played with my friends. Like many American girls, I loved playing with Barbie dolls. I would make clothes out of paper or scraps of material from a local seamstress.

In many ways, my life growing up in Nigeria was very sheltered. I had a stay-at-home mom who didn't have to work, and my dad made sure we didn't lack for anything. We were solidly middle class, which in Nigeria allowed chauffeurs and house help because services were so cheap. I almost never went anywhere without my mother or housemaid. I never went out without being chauffeured around. I was spoiled by my parents and popular with my friends. I had my music and a rich life of activities. Despite the unrest at home and in the streets, my life was comfortable and protected.

Little did I know then how abruptly and dramatically my life was about to change.

CHAPTER 2

STRENGTH THROUGH THE HARD TIMES

Having two such strong role models in my life and growing up in the Nigerian culture were vital to shaping my future. But there were two other factors that were also crucial, one filled with light and the other with darkness.

While education was important to my father, he also encouraged each of his children to pursue our passions outside of school. My oldest brother, for example, was so fascinated with politics and world affairs, every day my dad would bring him newspapers, and after dinner the two of them would sit together, surrounded by piles and piles of papers, and have long conversations about what was going on in the world. My passions were music and debate. From the time I was five years old, I loved singing and performing.

I was like a sponge, soaking up all the music around me and singing all day long. I had piano lessons, formed a singing group with my younger sisters, and did extracurricular music lessons. At school, I joined the choir and played the piano and the flute.

As passionate as I was about music, I had also always wanted to be an attorney, probably because I love to argue. In primary school, I joined the debate team at Aunty Ayo's Preparatory School and, because my brother had taught me how to get my point across and not back down, I always won for my class. When I was around nine years old, we even got the opportunity to compete on *Speak Out,* a televised educational program that aired every afternoon on NTA (Nigerian Television Authority) where kids from different schools came together to debate a selected topic.

Throughout Primary and Secondary School, I was always the youngest and smallest because I had excelled quickly and skipped ahead. I would always get teased or picked on for my size, but I was such a loudmouth I would forget I was the youngest. I had an extra-large ego and confidence to conquer whatever challenge or obstacle lay before me, and though I didn't know it then, this quality would become essential to my survival on the difficult journey on which I was about to embark at such a young age.

In Nigeria, Primary School begins around age five and typically goes for six years, and then there are three years of Junior Secondary School, popularly known as JSS, followed by another two to three years of Senior Secondary School, known as SSS. Along the way, there are promotional exams you must take to advance from one level to the next. It's not uncommon for students to sit these exams early and skip ahead according to their ability. I had skipped Year 6 of

Primary School and went straight to JSS, and then at fifteen, I took the standardized test administered by JAMB (Joint Admissions and Matriculation Board) for entrance into university. When you take the JAMB, there is a section where you list the university courses you are applying to in order of preference. I put down pre-law at University of Lagos where my father had studied as my first choice.

When the results of my exam came back, not only had I done well enough to get into most university programs, I had even scored higher than my older siblings who had taken the same exam. Most universities require a score between 180 and 200 out of a possible 400. I had scored 250. On the day they posted the list of names of those who had made it into their course, I went to the Faculty of Law at the University of Lagos and waited in line to see if my name was on the list. I remember looking around at the other hopeful students queuing up to find out if they had made it into their chosen programs, and I noticed that everyone was older, at least seventeen or eighteen, and far more confident than I was. For the first time in my life, I became aware of how much younger I was, and I began to feel intimidated. I was actually relieved when I found out my name wasn't on the list. While my score was impressive, especially for my age, it was a few points shy of what I needed to get into the pre-law program, which was one of the most competitive at the University of Lagos. I could easily have applied to another course or even petitioned to get into the pre-law program since my score was so close to the cutoff, but deep down I knew I wasn't ready.

Since we were always free to express ourselves with my father and to expect his support and guidance in return, that night I told him that I hadn't made it into the pre-law program and confided that I had started to feel that I wasn't quite ready to go to university. Knowing how ambitious I was and how advanced I was in my studies for my age, he agreed that I should take a year off and then re-take the exam the following spring. I would have plenty of time to decide if I still wanted to study law, or if I was better suited to another program. Or so I thought.

Looking back, we should have known that something was wrong when his car didn't pull up to the house at six o'clock sharp. You could set your watch by my father's return from work. He always came with sweets or some little surprise, and we looked forward to his return from work because this was our time with him, when we could tell him about what we had got up to that day or ask him for whatever little things we needed for the household.

At seven o'clock, he still wasn't home, and we thought it was very strange. My cousin said he thought he had seen my father's car pass by, and we kept expecting him to walk in the door any minute. An hour later, he still wasn't home, and we began to wonder if maybe he had gone to church or a meeting. Then, at around nine o'clock, there was a knock at the door. I remember my sisters and I were in my brother's bedroom, listening to 2Pac's *Changes*, which had just come out on the radio. My brother went to the door, and I recognized the voice of a man we had considered a family friend (I'll call him Dave) until he had fallen out with my brother a few months earlier. I was never told, nor did I ask, what the fight was about, but we had not seen Dave since he and my brother had fought, and I couldn't imagine what he could be doing at our home so late in the evening. I couldn't hear their conversation, but the feeling of hostility hung in the air like a dark, heavy cloud.

When I walked into the living room, I was met with an image that is forever burned into my memory. Dave was sitting down, and my brother was standing over him, shaking him by the shoulders and screaming over and over, "Where's my dad? Where's my dad?" I noticed that Dave had a bandaged finger, and my first thought was that he had gotten into some kind of accident. I ran to get my mom, who was outside. My brother was in a state of shock and could barely speak, but we were able to piece together that my dad had been shot and he was in the hospital.

My oldest brother, who was twenty-five and old enough to handle such things, went to the hospital with a few of our neighbors to assess the situation and learn what had happened to my father. As strong as my mother was in business, we felt we needed to protect her when it came to dangerous situations. It was decided that my older sister and I would stay home with her. By morning, every room in our house was filled with neighbors, cousins, distant relatives, and close friends who, in Nigeria, are always called Aunty and Uncle, who had come to offer support and see if there was any news of my father. My brother had come back from the hospital and reported that our father was going to be fine, so I was in high spirits thinking I would see him soon and our lives would return to normal.

Later in the day, my mom's best friend, Aunty Lizzy as we fondly called her, arrived and sat down on the couch with my mother in our living room. She had this look on her face that I didn't quite understand, but I assumed she was there to give my mother moral support for her husband being in the hospital. I decided to leave them alone and went outside. I remember passing neighbors sitting on the pavement in front of our house, and they all had these somber looks on their faces. I have no memory of where I was going or what I was about to do; I just remember that I had barely made it halfway around the side of the house when I heard my mother scream.

In that moment, I knew my father was gone.

To this day, we do not know what really happened on the night my father was killed. All we have is the account that Dave gave to the police, and I am resigned to the fact that we will never know the whole truth. According to his statement, and what he told us that night, Dave had been walking by the side of the road when my father, who must have been on his way home from work, recognized him and offered him a ride. They were driving across Third Mainland Bridge toward Lagos Island when a car overtook them and forced my father to pull over. Some men got out of the car and demanded that my father give them "the documents." When my father refused, Dave said one of them pulled out a gun and shot him in the chest. After they fired the first shot, he claimed he tried to shield my father, but the bullet grazed his finger, which was why it was bandaged that night, and went into my dad's abdomen, causing a mortal wound from which he would never recover.

My memories of the next few weeks are foggy and difficult to piece together. I don't think I was able to really process at the time what had happened. I just remember being really worried about my mother because with my father gone, she was now vulnerable to family members who had begun to descend upon our home like carrion birds circling a wounded animal.

While my father was a successful working class man, unfortunately, some of his siblings did not share his ambition or work ethic. He had been supporting them all for years, even putting his youngest brother through college. They were always coming to my father with their hands out, and of course my father never refused them. However, now that he was gone, instead of mourning the brother who had provided for them and their families all his life, they saw it as an opportunity to line their own pockets.

Wanting a piece of what my father had spent a lifetime working to build, they took it upon themselves to distribute his assets and property. In the days after he died, our neighbors came to us to say they had seen my uncles walking around our house taking inventory of all the equipment my mother had acquired over the years for her various businesses, like the ten standing freezers she used for her popsicle business, along with anything else we had of value. Money that should have gone to my mother was going missing left and right. On the day my father had been shot, he had entrusted one of his brothers to collect thirty thousand Nigerian Naira, which today would be about eighty-five dollars but back then was a huge sum of money, from a debt owed to him. Then, three days after he died, that brother announced out of the blue, "The craziest thing happened. I was on the bus on the day that Brother died, and I was so tired I said let me just lay my head on the chair in front of me…" Basically, his story was that he was carrying the money in a small duffel bag, and when he woke up, my father's money was gone. We all knew it was a lie, but my mother was not in a position to confront him.

Before the funeral, my father's body was brought to our house for the wake keeping so all of our family and friends in Lagos who had gathered for the viewing could keep vigil, sings songs, and say prayers. That day was the first time I ever saw my mother and stepmother together in the same room, although they never spoke a single word to one another. The few times I had seen her in my life before that, my stepmother had always seemed to me like a hostile person. If I went to her house to visit my father or half-siblings, she would not say hello or even acknowledge my presence. I blocked out the fact that this woman was a part of our family, because I didn't enjoy being around her.

Looking back now, I understand that this hostility probably came from a place of feeling defensive. They both loved my father, so I can only imagine how my stepmother felt that day, but she seemed very somber and looked like she was in a dark place. At least she pulled herself together. My mom, on the other hand, was so distraught she passed out several times and they had to get a doctor to administer an IV. My mother has never been the same since, and to this day she refuses to remarry.

We couldn't even trust my uncles to arrange for our father's body to be properly prepared for burial. His youngest brother, who when my father was alive had been almost like a son to him, had collected money from my mother (and then collected more money from my stepmother) for the embalming, but it wasn't done properly, if at all. When my grandmother died in 1995, she was embalmed in the village and even that was done better. At the wake keeping, I overheard people saying that his body was bloated and had already started to give off the smell of decomposition. I could not handle seeing my father like that, so I chose not to see his body. So not only had my uncles stolen money that rightfully belonged to my family, they robbed me of the chance to say goodbye to my father.

While the wake keeping was at our home in Lagos, the funeral was to be in my father's hometown just outside Owerri, capital of Imo State. Nigerians don't just bury you where you die. In our culture, you always get buried at home, and by home, I mean the village where your forefathers are from. So the next morning, about fifty of us—uncles and aunties, cousins, neighbors, friends, my stepmother and her children—all piled into two large buses to make the 545 kilometer (about 340 miles) journey to the village where my father was born.

I remember there being a lot of debate about how best to transport my father's body. They did not hire a hearse or any kind of transport for the casket, and initially my uncles tried to put it on the bus with us, wedged into the aisle with all the women and children, but in the end, it was deemed most practical to put my father in the luggage compartment. And so my beloved father, the man who had supported two loving wives, nine devoted children, and four greedy brothers, made his final journey home not in the dignified manner he deserved, but in the belly of a rented bus.

We arrived in Owerri the night before the burial. My father had a house in the village, but his brothers had taken over all the rooms, so my mother decided we should stay with a distant cousin who she trusted more than his other relatives. The next day about two hundred people—uncles and aunties, childhood friends, extended family members, people from the village—came to my father's funeral to pay their last respects. It was all planned by the village elders and my father's siblings, and at this point we were just spectators. Everyone was crying and wailing. Mourning in Nigeria is very intense. Death is taken very personally, like someone is against you and the enemy has won. It's seen as such a dark thing, and this was especially true in my father's case because he had been murdered.

I was really worried for my mother, because in some cases and certain cultures when a man dies, the wife is blamed.

Thankfully, no one openly blamed her, but the two days we spent in my father's village we felt like we were at their mercy. Having to deal with the greed and callous behavior of my father's family had a lot to do with shaping the woman I am today. I've seen the worst in people. I watched my uncles lose their dignity and their humanity because of their greed. They weren't capable of doing right by their brother, who raised them out of their circumstance and gave them a chance for a better life.

My father's death put an end to my ability to go to college and subsequently drove my family into poverty. Not only did we have to cope with the emotional devastation of his loss, we now had to learn to survive on our own. Where once our lives were filled with music and laughter, now there were days when we had little to eat. My mother, however, is a fighter. She wanted more for her children. Concerned about our future and also our physical safety, she was determined to raise the money to start sending us outside of Nigeria, where she felt we would be safe and have opportunities for a brighter future.

CHAPTER 3

WINNERS' PURE WATER

I f it hadn't been for my mother's entrepreneurial spirit, we would have been destitute. She may not have been educated like my father, but my mother had a sharp mind and keen eye for business opportunities. My father had given her a monthly allowance for the household, but for anything else she would have to go through her children because she was tired of asking him directly for money. She never liked the fact that she had been financially dependent on my father, and she always had a side hustle going.

She always positioned herself as manufacturer of goods. She started with selling food—bread, lollipops, ice cream, yogurt—that she made and sold from our home to workers in the area. When I was seven or eight, she took it to the next level and rented out a small spot on Lagos mainland and opened a mini restaurant. She cooked and served rice and stew dishes to people who would come during their lunch breaks to feast on her homemade delicacies.

Whenever my mother started up a new business, she would throw herself into it and gradually begin to neglect her responsibilities in the home. For the most part, my father would let it go, but when the balance would tip toward her putting too much attention to the business instead of the household, that was when my father would get mad. He especially did not like her preparing and selling food; at the time, it was considered petty trade. His mentality was that it was beneath him.

It was never long after one business would come to an end before she came up with something else to make and sell. She always had the fighting spirit to start a business, but it wasn't like our family depended on the income. There was never any serious balance or accounting, and usually by the time my father got worked up enough that he put his foot down, she was ready to move on and try something else anyway. For my mother, it was never about the money; it was about having something of her own. Once my father was gone and we had no financial support, this insatiable need for independence that compelled her to always be seeking out opportunities to manufacture a product and supply a market demand became our salvation.

In the year before my father was killed, she had started a bottled water business out of our home, or more accurately, a sachet water business. In Nigeria, we call it "pure water." Selling purified water blew up in Nigeria in 1990s because of a need throughout the country for affordable purified drinking water. The water purification infrastructure at that time could not keep up with the population explosion, so it was an attractive, and potentially lucrative, side hustle because practically anyone could start a pure-water business. All you really needed was a steady source of purified water and a sealing machine. There were vendors and street hawkers all over the city who sold purified water in sealed polyethylene pouches. It seemed like everyone was selling pure water, and it wasn't uncommon to see school-age children on the side of the road selling sachets of "pure water" to travelers, commuters, and harried drivers trying to weave through crawling traffic on the gridlocked roads of Lagos.

My mother spotted that need and got in on the ground floor. In the early days, I remember her going with a few of my aunties to meet with the distributors, who were supplying the armies of street hawkers and vendors around the city, to pitch her brand: Winners' Pure Water. She had no formal business training, but she was savvy enough to know that if she offered a free sample and undercut her competitors, she could entice prospective buyers to take a chance on her. She'd even offer to supply her water on credit to give them a chance to test the product, and ensure her bags didn't leak and the water was drinkable, with minimal risk. That was how she built her clientele. I didn't know it then, but I was learning at the hip of a true entrepreneur. She made mistakes along the way, but from those mistakes she learned better and more efficient ways to filter, pack, and store her water.

Demand for Winners' Pure Water grew quickly, and it wasn't long before my mother had distributors placing orders of fifty or even five hundred bags at a time. Her biggest challenge was finding portable ways of filtering and purifying the water, since she didn't have the land to dig a borehole or the specialized connection to the plumbing in our home necessary to deliver potable water directly into the bags. She set up a portable filtration system in the living room and kitchen of our home and packaged it in sealed bags printed with the name of her brand. She had no method for containing the overspill so there was always water everywhere. Our father would come back from work and the carpets were always soaking wet and there would be little puddles of water all over the house. Understandably, he was losing his mind. We didn't much care for it, either. I remember feeling extremely inconvenienced by it and complaining with my brothers and sisters to my dad about it. In order to pacify us, she took the filtration system out to the patio.

The filtration system she used in the beginning was basically a series of huge plastic kettle jugs that had heavy-duty filters built into their mouths. It was like having twenty giant teapot-shaped Britas set up all over our kitchen. These kettle jugs were filled with gallons of water taken directly from the faucet in our kitchen. She hired workers (there is always a ready supply of cheap labor in Nigeria) to help deliver the water from the jugs into the bags. Each worker, wearing the required white lab coat and hairnet, sat in front of a kettle jug which had been placed on a high stool, and they would continuously feed water into their bags. They would fill a bag and seal it, fill a bag and seal it, and on and on. When one jug was empty, there was always another ready to go. The system had to be as efficient as possible to avoid delays and allow her to fill and store as many bags as possible. Since my brothers and sisters and I all had to help out, I had done it myself hundreds of times, and I assure you it was a tedious process.

By the time she had moved out to the enclosed patio, the business had started to have a structure of its own. She was getting so many orders that she doubled her workforce and had water sealers who bagged the water and packers who were hired just to arrange and pack the sachets into bigger bags of twelve working around the clock. We actually had people working in twelve-hour overnight shifts out of our home. What gave her an edge over her competition was that she already had a dedicated car and a driver as part of her household allowance from my father. That afforded her the opportunity to meet with buyers throughout the city and expand her customer base, and she was also able to offer them free delivery of her product. So she was smart enough to use our family resources to give her an edge over her competitors.

Even though my dad was frustrated by this new venture, he didn't hate it as much as when she was selling food. His biggest problem was the inconvenience and wear and tear on the house. She was still operating from our patio when he was killed, but I think he would have helped her move into a commercial space. Once he was gone, Winners' Pure Water was our only source of income, so when she got reported to the Nigerian Food and Drug Administration, instead of shutting down like she might have done when my dad was alive, my mother built up the patio walls so people could no longer see in and she could operate in private. Within two years, she had saved enough money to move the business from our home to a commercial location. She bought an empty plot of land inside the subdivision where we lived, found a borehole, built a warehouse from the ground up, and installed an industry-grade filtration system.

Looking back, I can appreciate Winners' Pure Water for the ingenious hustle that it was, but back then I just saw it as this annoying side business that I hated with all my heart. It demanded the lion's share of my mother's time and attention and took over our home. It was such a mess. Now that I am running a business of my own and understand all the challenges she was facing. I wish my mother had better guidance back then because she could have taken the business so much further. For years, it was the only thing that kept us afloat, but in the end, she was undone by two factors that plague all small business owners: brand loyalty and poor management.

When she got to the point where she had to go official and trademark her company name, someone had already taken Winners' Pure Water so she couldn't legally trade under that name. She had no choice but to operate under a new name, resulting in confusion for customers who were now reluctant to buy from her because they didn't trust that it was the same company. She lost her brand identity, and her customer trust went with it. The same thing happened to Coca Cola when they changed their design.

Her second fatal mistake was in trusting someone else to run the day-to-day administrative side of her businesses. Not long after my father was killed, she was approached by a man in her church who claimed to have several businesses of his own, although she never verified if that was true. He told her, "God told me to come help you." Those were the magic words. My mother was so naïve that she blindly handed over the reins to this man. She stopped checking in and let him handle the business for her, and he ran it into the ground.

While all of this was going on, my mother was mourning the loss of her husband and trying to support six children. In the months after my father was killed, there was still so much confusion and uncertainty surrounding his death. We had no idea why he was shot or if they would be coming for us. We were all confused and didn't know what to think.

One of my aunties lived in the Republic of Benin, a tiny Francophone country on the western border of Nigeria, about a two-hour drive from Lagos. We had heard so many good things about Cotonou, the city where she lived, so we begged my mother to ask if we could stay with her for a while. It had been such a painful year that we needed to get away from all the bad energy of losing my dad. With my mother wanting us to have something productive to do, six months after my dad was killed, it was decided that I would go with my two younger sisters to stay with my aunty.

After a few months, my sisters went back to Nigeria to finish Secondary School, but I stayed on with my aunty to continue learning French and enrolled in a computer school. This was around 1999 and into the early 2000s. Computers were common, but the internet was still very much a novelty. I could browse the internet, but I didn't know how to touch type or use basic software. I didn't know it then, but this early training would become the foundation for skills that would prove essential when I finally had control of my life and decided to start my first ecommerce business.

The Republic of Benin is a beautiful country. We were living by the beach, and I made friends and had a lot of fun. I was traveling back and forth between Lagos and Cotonou, but after a while I felt like it was time to get serious about my life. I wanted to get my degree and make something of my life. I decided to go back home to Nigeria and apply for a student visa to the U.S. At that time, for so many young Nigerians the goal was to move outside of the country. The U.S., England, China, even the Republic of Benin had more options because we just felt like other countries were better managed. It was unfortunate for us because it is a huge metropolis, so we already had the experience of a developing country, but we were not living like a developing country. It was so frustrating to be aware of technology but not be able to use it.

It didn't take long to get my visa, which was shocking. Now everything is done electronically, but at that time you had to physically go down to the embassy to fill out the forms and pay your application fee. It wouldn't be easy, because they'll deny you and not even tell you why. I was prepared for the worst, but within a few weeks, I got a letter via courier that I had been given an appointment for an interview. I went to the American embassy, and I don't know if I was charismatic or what, but I got my visa that same day.

My brother got in touch with his childhood best friend who had moved to the U.S. a few years earlier and was now living in Atlanta, Georgia. The Nigerian couple he was staying with had a room I could rent until I found something more permanent. My mom scraped together what little she had and borrowed the rest to pay for my airfare, which wasn't easy for her, and just like that, at the age of eighteen, I arrived in America with little more than one hundred dollars in my pocket, two sets of clothing, and two pairs of shoes. I had no plan. I didn't know how I was going to pay for school or earn money to survive. I just knew that I was coming to the land of plenty.

CHAPTER 4

A TRAPPED IMMIGRANT IN THE LAND OF PLENTY

For those who have never been an immigrant or experienced the shock of being totally immersed in a foreign culture, it is hard for me to paint a picture of what it was like stepping off the airplane and into a different life. Learning how to navigate this new world was difficult to say the least, but doing that without the support of family and friends made it even harder and lonelier. That was where my determination to survive and thrive kicked in. I felt that I had no option but to succeed, and in the end, that was what always raised me up in my darkest hours. Unfortunately, there would be no shortage of those on the road ahead.

When I arrived in the U.S. as a young girl full of hope and optimism for my future, I knew nothing about Atlanta, least of all that the neighborhood I'd be living in was rampant with crackheads, homeless people, and petty crime. My brother's friend picked me up from the airport, and as we drove through South East Atlanta, I remember thinking that the streets looked so clean and quiet compared to the noisy, congested, overpopulated streets of Lagos Island. When we pulled up to the gated apartment complex on Cleveland Avenue where he was living, he punched in a security code and said to me, "Don't let the automatic gates fool you. This is the hood." I remember thinking it was funny this kind of place was considered "the hood" in America, but after living there for a few months, I began to understand what he meant. If you ask anyone from Atlanta, they will tell you about Cleveland Avenue. In recent years, the neighborhood has begun to change because of gentrification, but at the time there were vacant and boarded-up homes everywhere you looked. To this day, one in five households are run by single mothers, and nearly 75 percent of children live below the poverty level. Robberies, vandalism, drugs, gang shootings, police brutality...Cleveland Avenue has it all. I never expected to see this level of despair in the U.S. It was shocking to see able-bodied people on the street begging for money. At the time, I thought surely there must be enough work for everyone in America. Of course, this was unrealistic and naïve, but stepping off that plane, I truly believed I had arrived in the land of plenty.

My brother's friend was renting a room from a Nigerian couple, and even though they didn't know me, they had offered to take me in as well. In Nigeria, people are very open-handed, and they will welcome you into their home. This is especially true among our expatriate communities abroad. I don't think I was able to fully appreciate the sacrifice they were making for me at the time. I was a young girl full of energy and excitement. I'm sure I rubbed them the wrong way because I was a ball of enthusiasm, and they had been in the U.S. longer and were more cynical. I felt like I was ready to conquer the world, but they were telling me to slow down. I was sure I knew everything. That was *me* all the way. I thought within a week I'd have a car and a job, and the harsh reality of my situation as a trapped immigrant began to sink in almost immediately. My employment options were severely limited. Without a driver's license, I didn't have the freedom to travel around the city on my own. I couldn't apply for financial aid, so my dream of a college education was on hold indefinitely. My mother had borrowed money to help pay for my plane ticket, which was several thousand dollars, a small fortune for a widowed mother struggling to support children back home. If I failed, I would have wasted money that was borrowed in the first place. Giving up and going back home to Nigeria was not an option.

With no money, no job, and no means of transportation, I was totally dependent on my brother's friend and the couple that had taken me in. I was so desperate that when my brother's friend told me he had a friend who owned a laundromat on Cleveland Avenue and they were looking to hire someone, I jumped at the opportunity. I spent my first few months in America sitting at the counter of a laundromat and making change for customers who came in to use the machines. It wasn't my dream job, but it paid six dollars an hour and got me out of our cramped and crowded apartment. Then one day, a bunch of teenage boys came into the laundromat. I figured they were up to something when they all went into the bathroom together, so I sat at the register trying to protect the cash. When they finally came out, they came to the counter to tell me that someone had messed up the toilet and the water was overflowing. I rushed to the bathroom and saw that they had filled up the toilet with paper towels. There was water and paper all over the floor. When I returned to my post, the cash register was open and all the money was gone. I noticed footprints on the counter and realized that the boys had purposely created a distraction and then jumped over the counter while I was in the bathroom dealing with the mess. I called my boss and the police, and that was the end of that job.

Meanwhile, I had been getting sicker and sicker, and I didn't know why. I felt weak and was suffering from agonizing headaches. Since I had no health insurance, I went to a low-income clinic in West End Atlanta. They did blood work and ran some tests, and it turned out I was suffering from a hormonal imbalance. In Nigeria, we don't use hormones or chemicals in our livestock; therefore, the sudden change in diet was wreaking havoc on my body. They put me on birth control to regulate my hormones and told me to avoid eating chicken, which thankfully fixed the problem almost immediately.

If only there had been a pill I could have taken to cure my loneliness and isolation. The couple I was living with had a Nigerian friend who always came around. The wife was an excellent cook, and he would come during lunch to hang out and eat traditional Nigerian dishes, like fufu and okra soup or jollof rice with fried chicken. He was a nice guy and always spoke about his church. Recalling how after my dad passed I had found such comfort in our church in Lagos, the next time he came around, I asked him about it, and he offered to take me. That Sunday, he came and picked me up with his wife and kids and took me to his church.

It was a typical Sunday service, with singing and a preacher who delivered his sermon for the day. I had always gone to church with my mother back in Nigeria, but this was warmer and more welcoming. I liked it right away, especially because the service was short, only two hours, compared to my mother's Pentecostal Baptist church where Sunday services could last up to six hours. For the first time since I had left Lagos and arrived in Atlanta, I actually felt at home. After the service, a group of young people came over to introduce themselves. They were super friendly and asked if I wanted to hang out and grab lunch the next day. I was so excited. This was what I had been longing for all these months, to have a connection and friendships with people my own age. The next day, I met them at the McDonald's at the junction of Cleveland Avenue and Browns Mill Road. As soon as we sat down, they whipped out their Bibles. I don't know what I expected Americans my age to be like, but that did surprise me a little. I didn't necessarily think of it as a study group, although that's what it was. I just thought they must *love* reading their Bibles. I wanted consistency and companionship, and I felt these people would be a good influence in my life. Besides, my mother would love hearing that I was getting serious about religion. Like a lot of churches, the Atlanta Church of Christ was divided into life stages, with dedicated ministries for teens, singles, students, and married couples. It's set up this way for like-minded people within the same church to gather during the week, for Bible study and movie nights. You're with people your own age, so you're motivated to keep going to church. It was close-knit and every bit what I needed at that time. Good, kind people who made me feel like I belonged. We started meeting once or twice a week to read our Bibles, and my life quickly began to revolve around my newfound community.

The church became my gateway into life as an American and a way out of the situation I was in. After I left the laundromat, the couple I was living with got me a job working for a man they knew who ran a car service out of his home. On my second day at work, he took me out in his car to teach me how to navigate the neighborhood. Since he seemed friendly, I got to chatting with him about my living situation and confided that the wife and I weren't getting along. After a little while, he pulled over. Then he leaned over and started to kiss me, feel on me, and grab at my breasts. I couldn't believe this was actually happening. He was my boss. He was *married*. I didn't know how I was supposed to react. I was frightened and repulsed by his touch, but I needed the job. I could barely move or breathe, but I kept my head together and decided to play to his ego to get myself out of there. I pushed him off me, and I told him that I like him, but I was a good Christian girl and we had to wait. Thankfully he backed off, but it was only a matter of time before he came after me again, and the next time he might not take no for an answer.

When I got home, I told my brother's friend what had happened. He was outraged, and the next day he went to the man's house to confront him. Of course, he denied he had done anything, but even worse, he went to the couple I was living with and turned them against me. He told them that I was spoiled and ungrateful and that I had been complaining to him about my living situation. They completely ignored what he had done and were angry with me for causing trouble. They insisted I keep my mouth shut and go back to work. As I got older, I began to understand why there was so much tension between the wife and me. I was young woman with no attachments living in her home. I was also opinionated and strong willed, so it was easy for her to believe I was a troublemaker. As confident and fearless as I was back then, I was also indebted to this couple for taking me in. I began to feel as though I had no choice but to go back to work for this man.

Every woman who has ever been the victim of a sexual predator, and sadly there are so many of us out there, will recognize the mixture of anger and shame that consumes you when a man in a position of authority uses his power to pressure you into a sexual situation. I began to wonder, *Was it my fault? Was I wearing something too low cut or revealing? Did I do something to provoke his advances?* Thankfully, I didn't keep what had happened to myself. I confided in a woman I met through the church, who was older and American. When I told her that the couple I was living with wanted me to go back to work for that man, she explained to me that I had rights.

"Do not go back there if you do not feel safe, and don't allow anyone to make you think otherwise," she told me.

I found the strength I needed in her words and decided that, no matter what, I was not going to lower my standards to go back into that environment. That was the beginning of my initiation into the American mentality. I was no longer just a young girl from Nigeria who didn't understand I had rights. I was a strong, independent woman with a supportive community of friends to lift me up in moments of doubt.

I stood my ground and refused to go back to work for that man. However, I still needed a job, and the truth was, I didn't have many options. My brother's friend worked at a gas station on Cleveland Avenue, not far from where we were living. He convinced his boss to hire me, so he really went above and beyond and looked out for me like I was his sister. That was the first job I had in Atlanta where I had a consistent-enough income that I was actually able to send money back home to my mother to pay off her debt for my airline ticket. I was even able to set aside a little bit of money each week to begin saving toward the day I would be able to move out of that apartment.

Working at the gas station on Cleveland Avenue was my true introduction to life in the 'hood. I remember times when a customer who frequented the place suddenly stopped coming around. I would ask after them only to find out they had been shot and killed. It seemed like everyone on Cleveland Avenue was either trying to survive or looking to get high. The gas station was an easy target for thieves. Sometimes they'd work in a group; while one of them distracted me, the others would be filling their pockets. Other people would come in on their own, go directly back to the beer section of the fridge, take out a six-pack and quietly walk toward the register like they were about to pay. As soon as they got close enough to the door, they'd bolt.

Then there were the crackheads and the drunks stationed right outside the gas station every night, begging for money. As soon as they had scraped together a dollar, they'd come right in to buy a bottle of beer. When that was gone, they were right back to begging for the next dollar. The saddest was always the young mothers who came in to shoplift with their children. There were nights I wanted to scream from heartbreak and frustration for all these lost souls. Thank God we never had a gun drawn on us, but we always lived in fear of it. I hated working at that gas station with every fiber of my being. Although this wasn't where I was supposed to be, it was a good job with a steady income, so I prayed for patience and found a way to make myself comfortable with it.

Within a year, I had earned enough money to pay back my mom. By then, I had joined the campus ministry at the church and had formed a tight group of girlfriends who were all American. I felt like if I wanted to be around Nigerians, I should have stayed home. I wanted to fully experience the American lifestyle and deliberately put myself in situations where I was forced to step outside of my comfort zone and learn about the country I was in. These girls paid their own rent and took care of themselves. The minute I had saved up enough money from my wages at the gas station, I left the apartment on Cleveland Avenue and moved into a three-bedroom townhouse with these girls in the suburban neighborhood of North Druid Hills.

Finally, I was out of the 'hood and living on my own terms, with people my own age. I loved my new roommates. One was a gamer type, who was a huge movie buff and introduced me to American cinema. The other was a California girl who had moved to Georgia as a teenager. Her mom was American, and her dad was from St. Croix. She was dating a Nigerian guy, so she wanted to learn everything she could about Nigerian culture, and that was how we bonded. Our third roommate was nice also, but she was older so we didn't have as much overlap because she was in the singles ministry.

I kept working at the gas station, and most nights my brother's friend would pick me up or drop me off at the house. On nights he couldn't, I would have to take the bus home. A few months after I moved in, I took the bus home from work. It was dark, and as I was walking home, I heard footsteps behind me. I immediately felt paranoid that someone was following me, but I thought it was because I'm from Lagos, where you always have to be aware and alert; you don't play when it comes to your safety. We had all kinds of crazies, and you had to be sharp. I looked over my shoulder and saw a man walking about twenty feet behind me. I picked up my pace, but every time I turned back around, he was a few feet closer. When I was within a block of the house, a car drove by and honked. I looked up, and it was my older roommate. She slowed down a little bit, honked again, and then parked her car in front of our house. By that point, I was practically running, digging in my purse for my keys, and by the time I got to the door, I already had them in my hand. I opened the door and quickly shut it behind me. When I had caught my breath, my roommate told me she had noticed the man walking behind me and that was why she had honked. So I wasn't being paranoid after all! An hour later, I was in the kitchen, and I noticed someone peeking in through the window. I screamed, and that must have scared him off because when I looked again he was gone. I never got a sense of what he looked like, but his shadow haunted me from that day on.

A few months went by, and I tried to put the memory of that night in the back of my mind. Then one night, one of my closest girlfriends from the church came over to hang out. She was half Nigerian, and we had bonded over our shared culture. Along with my roommates, we had formed a tight-knit clique. That night we fell asleep on the futon in the living room, but I woke up at around one o'clock in the morning feeling very afraid. I thought I was being paranoid and didn't want to wake my friend and decided to go upstairs to my bedroom. I fell back into a deep sleep and dreamt I was back in Nigeria with my friend. We were in my primary school, and for some reason we were being chased by a lot of boys. Then they stopped chasing me and they were just chasing her. I heard my friend screaming, and suddenly I wasn't in the dream anymore. I was back in my house in Atlanta, and I could hear a commotion and thudding coming from downstairs. I ran out of my room, and my friend was sitting at the bottom of the steps, crying and screaming for her mother.

By that point my other roommates had heard her screams as well and had come out of their rooms to see what was going on. My friend couldn't speak; she just kept crying and calling out for her mom. When we saw the blood on the steps where she was sitting, the reality of what had happened to her began to sink in. An intruder had broken into the house and raped her while the rest of us were asleep upstairs. We immediately called 911, and when the police arrived, they examined my friend with a rape kit, which was as traumatic and invasive as what had just happened to her. Then they questioned everyone in the house. I told them about the man who had followed me home a few months earlier, but because I never saw his face, I wasn't able to provide them with a description that could link him to the man who had attacked my friend.

They never caught the intruder. I'll never know if it was the same man or what it was that woke me up that night and sent me upstairs, but I live with the memory of that night every day of my life. Because of the assault, none of us felt safe in that house anymore, so that night we packed up all our belongings and never looked back. I moved from one temporary situation to another, always looking over my shoulder and always afraid to be alone. Even if the place I was living in was on the second floor, I was afraid to leave the door unlocked or even keep the window open.

A few weeks later, the stress of everything that had happened triggered the hormonal imbalance I had been suffering from after I first arrived in Atlanta, and this time it came back with a vengeance. I was so sick I ended up in the hospital for five days, and by then I'd missed so much work that I lost my job at the gas station. Thus, two years after I first arrived in America, I found myself with no job and nowhere to live.

CHAPTER 5

THE END OF THE RAINBOW

E ven on my darkest days, and there was no shortage of those, I woke up every morning thinking, *I'm in America!* I never let myself forget that or take it for granted. I had an unshakable belief that I had come to the U.S. for a purpose and that if I worked hard enough, I could conquer any obstacle in my path and achieve every goal I set for myself. I wanted to go to college and get my degree. I wanted to fall in love and get married. I wanted to be a successful businesswoman. Despite all that had happened, I truly believed, and still do to this day, that I had left Nigeria to fulfill those dreams.

After I moved out of the house in North Druid Hills, I must have moved six times in four months. I would get settled into an apartment, and then the leasing office would get wind that one too many people were living there and I'd have to move again. Finally, I met a woman through the church who owned a house in Decatur, just outside of Atlanta, and she rented me a room. It was a relief to finally feel settled somewhere, but I still needed a way to pay rent and support myself. I was out of work for a few weeks, but I did not live on much at the time. My rent was only about two hundred and fifty dollars per month, and thankfully I had saved enough to keep me going until I found work.

One day while I was walking around the neighborhood, I came across an African-owned salon that specialized in braiding and hair extensions. I figured I had nothing to lose at this point and decided to see if they had any openings. The owner of the salon was from Senegal, a Francophone country, so I used the French I had learned in the Republic of Benin to ask if I could apply for a position as a hair stylist. At the time, she was braiding extensions into a woman's hair. She handed me one and said, "Okay, show me what you can do." The only actual experience I had styling hair was from playing with my dolls as a young girl, but I figured *she* didn't have to know that. I braided a couple of pieces of hair into the back of this poor woman's head, and honestly it was a hot mess back there. Either she saw some potential or more likely she took pity on me, because she decided to take me on and train me. The fact that I spoke French definitely helped, because if I had gone in there speaking English asking for a job, even if I was African, she probably would never have hired me—especially when I had no idea what I was doing.

The salon was definitely a step up from the gas station. The clientele was a lot better behaved, and I never had a bad experience with a single customer. The women who worked at the salon, on the other hand, could be a handful.

We were all loud and boisterous, with big personalities and fiery tempers. I was the only Nigerian working there. Most of the women came from Senegal, like the owner, and they all spoke Wolof. Since there were a few women from the Ivory Coast and one from Cameroon, the common language was French. I didn't speak as well as the other women, but I had learned enough in Republic of Benin to hold my own. Over the next few years, they trained me as a stylist, and eventually I graduated from the back of the head to the front.

Outside of work, my life had become completely immersed in the church. On top of Sunday service, we had a mid-week service every Wednesday that was mandatory; you were encouraged to turn down jobs that required you to work on Sundays or Wednesdays. There was a movie night once a week, parties on Saturdays, and Bible study with new recruits during the week. On top of all that, we were required to make time to sit with our *discipler* to confess our sins. We were also expected to have quiet time (prayer) every morning or we'd be falling short of our Christian duty. At some point, I started to realize we were following a kind of syllabus. When I went to church, people in the congregation would ask, "Are you still *studying* or are you member?" Gradually, it began to sink in: I was not just reading my Bible for the love of scripture; I was "studying" to become a member. It was an initiation process through which they were building a belief system. It had its value, but there's always a darker side, and over time what began as a safe haven became like a prison.

I was trained to question other people's beliefs and to always be asking, "Where is it in the Bible?" I could no longer make decisions without getting permission from the church. In fact, I was not allowed to have friends outside of the church members. I was not permitted to visit other churches. I remember that one time, when I visited another church for midweek service, three people sat me down to discuss why I had chosen to visit another church. Every decision I made had to be approved by the church first, which sometimes included what type of job to accept or when to cut off friends and family members. The goal became recruiting new members rather than getting to know people for who they were. Whenever I met people, I was desperately finding ways to get them to join the church as instructed by the leaders.

As my life became more and more deeply enmeshed with the church, my mind was being crafted and conditioned to question everything I had believed in before. Gradually, this began to undermine my connection to the outside world and ultimately to my family and culture. I even began to question my own mother, who has always been a devout and righteous Christian woman. If everyone outside the church is wrong, then obviously the only people I can trust are in the church. That kind of thinking shatters your strong belief in the matriarch of your family, and you begin to challenge *her* ideas and *her* belief system, which was something I never foresaw happening when I first joined the church.

When you are recruited into this kind of community, it becomes your life, and when it's time for you to come back to your senses, you're never the same again. When you look right, left, and center, everyone around you is from the church, and there is no longer any balance. I am still grateful that I had the foundation of the church to protect me. I was a teenager when I arrived in the U.S., and they guided and protected me when I needed it most. I was shallow minded and not a deep thinker, and they taught me to question the world around me. This way of thinking is what helped me to break free. I had learned to question, and so I began questioning the church.

Eventually, I enrolled part time at Georgia Perimeter College to study accounting and took a full-time job working the customer service desk at a public storage facility, but in those first few months, I was at home and I actually had some time to dream and plan for what the future might hold. I always had this idea in the back of my mind that I wanted to have a business of my own, to build and grow something from the ground up. I would spend hours every day and night on the computer, scouring the internet, following link after link, watching webinar after webinar. I didn't know it then, but I was learning and absorbing the lessons that would later form the foundation of my ecommerce business.

I could not shake this dream of owning my own business, and it became a source of constant friction in my first marriage. If I was on the computer doing research, James would bark at me that I was wasting my time when I should be focused on looking for work. I would try to explain, "Of course I'll get a job, but what if we also work toward starting our own business someday?" He didn't like the idea of taking that kind of risk, and that was a huge disconnect between us.

It was also becoming clear to me that he didn't have any appreciation for my culture. For our wedding, I had made him a traditional Nigerian outfit, a black Dashiki with gold embroidery which we would wear to the reception after the ceremony, but he hated it. It took almost three days of constant fighting and persuasion before he finally gave in and agreed to wear it.

That should have been my first red flag. Whenever I cooked Nigerian food, he would complain about the smell. To be fair, there are some Nigerian dishes that definitely do have an intense aroma just like many other dishes from around the world, but he even turned his nose up at the more mainstream dishes that you would find in Nigerian restaurants in Atlanta. He also never wanted to travel out of the country, which was totally crazy to me. If I suggested we go to Nigeria to visit my family, he would say, "Oh, hell no." He was simply not open to trying anything new. I found myself questioning why he would marry a Nigerian if he was not open to other cultures.

After we got married, I decided to leave the mind controlling church once and for all. I begged James to leave with me, and he did, but deep down we both knew his heart was still there. I still strongly believed in God, and I started going to a Nigerian church. I felt like I had totally forgotten who I was. I needed to reconnect with my roots to regain confidence in myself. Gradually, I began to connect with who I was and where I came from.

During this whole process of leaving the church, I was reevaluating my life and trying to call back the confident young woman I was when I had arrived in Atlanta. James and I needed healing and counseling, because we had just come out of what we considered a mind control situation, but he didn't want to go. Once our lives stopped revolving around the church, it became painfully clear to us that we did not have anything in common. We didn't know each other at all because we never had the chance to get to know one another outside the church.

At the end of the day, the biggest problem we had was that we did not share the same goals in life. I wanted to run my own business, and I always knew I would. He wanted nothing to do with that, and worse, he wanted me to give up on it as well.

Since neither of us was happy, we made the difficult and painful decision to end the marriage. That first year was a lot of crying and struggling, trying to fight what was happening. I sunk into a depression. I was now living on my own, and on my own terms, for the first time in my life, but it was also a period of deep emotional turmoil. I remember times I would start crying out of nowhere and not know why. I felt extremely lonely and very alone.

My family didn't support our decision to end the marriage. No one did, because on the surface it seemed like a picture-perfect situation. However, no one was aware of the inner turmoil of living with someone who rejects everything that you are: my culture, my origin, my family. James saw my culture as beneath him. He wanted nothing to do with Nigeria or Nigerian people.

Although I was absolutely terrified, it was a risk I had to take if I was ever going to live the life I wanted to lead. It's the same principal in business: if you're not a little bit scared, you're not aiming high enough. You have to take risks. It's the only way to build and grow, in life and in business. If you keep doing the same thing, your life becomes static. If you pursue what makes you passionate, everything you do will be infused with the energy of that passion.

CHAPTER 6

WHEN ONE DOOR CLOSES...

That first year on my own was an emotional roller-coaster. A couple of months before my marriage ended, I had started a new job working in the mortgage department at Chase Bank, and I had moved to Duluth to be closer to work. I was in a new job, a new city, a new apartment, and had a new life. It was the fresh start I needed, but in many ways, it was a very lonely time. My mind had been so conditioned by the church to being a part of a community that I had to completely relearn how to be on my own. I would get home from work, and for the first time in my life, there was no one there. Being alone with nothing but my own thoughts forced all the emotions I had been suppressing to the surface, and it was overwhelming at times.

That first Christmas on my own was especially difficult. By then, I'd been living on my own for eight months, and to escape the loneliness I had started going out dancing with my girlfriends. One of them was also going through a divorce, and we were able to support one another through the process. I'd never been dancing before, and I discovered that I loved it. When I was on the dance floor, I could lose myself in the music and be young and free. As painful as it was to walk away from my marriage, there was also a big part of me that felt liberated to finally to be on my own path. I had gone from my mother's home, to the church, to a marriage, and I'd never really had the freedom to make my own choices.

Still struggling to adjust to this new life, when one of my girlfriends wanted to go out dancing on Christmas Eve, I almost didn't go. I wasn't in the mood to be social, but I agreed to accompany her to one of the African Spots we went to regularly. Not long after we got there, out of the corner of my eye I noticed this guy looking at me from across the dance floor. I remember thinking, *Who's this creep in the corner looking at me?* I definitely did not give him a friendly look back, but he came over anyway and offered to buy me a drink. I told him no, but he didn't give up. He introduced himself as Mansour and started chatting relentlessly about how he'd been to Africa. I was there to listen to music and dance, and here's this guy going on and on about his African trip. I assumed he must have gone as a tourist or perhaps as a student and was telling me a story to try and impress me. I decided if I was stuck listening to his stories, I might as well allow him to buy me and my friend a drink.

For the rest of the night, Mansour would not leave my side. After we left the African Spot, a group of us ended up at IHOP, where I overheard him speaking Broken English to his cousin. That got my attention. It sounded like Nigerian Pidgin English, but I also noticed a little bit of a difference. I was very confused because he was American, but he was conversing in Pidgin English like he was speaking his native language. I started wondering, did he grow up in Africa? Who taught him how to speak Broken English? It was such a trip. At that point, I was hooked. I wanted to know more about this mysterious person who spoke my native language with such ease.

At the end of the night, we exchanged numbers. When he called me the next day, we talked for hours. I was fascinated to learn that he had actually lived all over Africa. His parents were American and had met in Senegal as exchange students. He was born in Detroit, but when he was five years old, they had moved to Africa, first to Senegal for a few years and then The Gambia, which is right next door, for a few more years. Then they moved to Ghana, which is where he spent most of his time in Africa and where he had learned to speak Pidgin English. The more we spoke, the more we found we had in common. We had even moved from Africa to Atlanta the exact same month and year. Since moving back to the U.S., he had taken over running his stepfather's trucking business and spent most of his time on the road behind the wheel of a fifty-three-foot 18-wheeler truck, driving back and forth across the country.

At the end of our conversation, we talked about going out for New Year's Eve. Surprisingly, I was really looking forward to it. This was the first time since my marriage had ended that I had considered going out on a date. It was a huge deal for me to be putting myself out there again, but I thought this guy might actually be worth getting to know better. New Year's Eve came...and nothing. I was ready for a magical evening with this amazing guy, but he didn't call. I had turned down plans to go out with friends, and by the time I realized I had been stood up, it was too late to go out. I sat home alone that whole night in my empty apartment, feeling angry, frustrated, and disappointed.

I wanted to call Mansour and let him have it, but I checked myself. I decided to play it cool and be patient. I figured when he got back out on the road, he'd get lonely, and then he would remember me and give me a call, which was exactly what happened. When he called two days later, I was ready. I had it all planned in my head. I was going to be cool and aloof. I was going to tell him that I wasn't interested in hanging out with him anymore. I was going to calmly tell him to please never call me again. But no, I couldn't hold back. As soon as I got on the phone with him, I let loose. I told him he was selfish and insensitive. I told him that I deserved better. I told him that he was a jerk for ruining my night. I was done toning myself down.

As I was ranting and telling him about himself, it occurred to me that Mansour wasn't rushing to get off the phone. I was shocked because I expected him to be like, "Girl, you are way too much," and hang up. But he didn't. He listened to everything I had to say, and when I was done unleashing my fury, he explained that he had spent New Year's Eve with his family and that he had forgotten that we'd talked about getting together. He was apologetic and understanding. He didn't run away, and that was really impressive to me. I think he was impressed that I spoke my mind, that I wasn't playing games and didn't shy away from telling him what I thought.

The thing is, I am aware I can be a little bit too much. I have a big personality, I'm loud, and I'm opinionated. That can be a lot for some people to handle. I had spent so many years suppressing that side of myself to make other people happy. With the church and in my marriage, I felt like I always had to be on my best behavior, but I was finally at a point in my life where I was done pretending to be something I wasn't. I realized while I was on the phone with Mansour that I didn't feel pressure to be perfect or on my best behavior. He liked that I was loud and opinionated. He respected and was attracted to the real me.

From that moment on, we knew we were meant to be together. Our biggest challenge was the fact that his work took him out of town so much. When he wasn't on the road, we were inseparable. We were always talking about getting the life we really wanted and turning our dreams into reality. We were both on a safe and predictable track at work, and we were reminded of the life we truly wanted to live. We started to feel uncomfortable in our comfortable jobs. Mansour was sick of driving a truck and always being out on the road. It was a big leap for him to leave the family business, but with my encouragement, he was able to parlay the skills he'd acquired running the family trucking business into landing a good management position at another job.

It's ironic that our relationship would begin with me being angry with Mansour for letting me down because he is truly a loyal and supportive partner. In many ways, it was a good test for me, because I made the decision to be true to myself from the beginning. Our relationship is an equal partnership. We have the same goals and are very much in sync with each other. Before we met, I thought I would never get married again, but once I found myself in a relationship with someone that truly loved, understood, and respected me and my culture, it was only natural for us to get married and become a family.

I was still going to school and working at the bank part time. It would have been easy to stay where I was. I was learning new skills, meeting new people, and I loved the steady income. But the more we talked about what we really wanted in life, the more I began to dream about being part of something bigger than myself. Honestly, Mansour probably did think I was crazy when I first told him I wanted to start my own business, but fortunately he believed in me and trusted my instincts, and I'm sure it didn't hurt that he also thought I was cute. Our story has been one of love, support, and feeding off of each other's energy.

With every conversation we had, I felt a stronger need to turn our shared dream into action. As I began charting our destiny, creating an ecommerce business became the forefront of my focus. I knew *how* to sell; what I didn't know was *what* to sell. It had to be a product that would inspire my creativity and energy. I decided to start with what I knew: hair extensions. From working at the salon, I had learned there was a huge market for selling human hair for weaving. I had heard there were small businesses out there making a lot of money importing hair from countries like India, Europe, Indonesia, and China. I went straight into research mode. I spent every waking moment scouring the internet, learning everything I could about where to buy and how to sell hair extensions. Indian and Brazilian hair was the most sought after at the time, and confident this was a product we could sell, Mansour and I dipped into our savings and invested about two thousand dollars in purchasing our initial inventory.

At that point, I knew nothing about building a website. I actually called the customer service department at GoDaddy, which was the dominant web hosting company at the time, and they walked me through everything from logging in, to uploading photos, to setting up a shopping cart so I could process credit cards through the website, create customer accounts with order history, and a catalog that housed products where customers could browse. It took me a solid twelve hours just to figure out how to set up the site, but once it was up and running, I felt such pride in my work.

To promote the business locally, I printed out fliers and literally went door-to-door handing them out at salons and putting them under people's doors. I was hustling like a Nigerian, trying to reach everyone everywhere. That's the beauty of the side hustle. It's all about passion and dedication. When you love what you do, you put everything you have into it. What I understood fundamentally going into this venture is that success and obsession go hand in hand. You have to eat, sleep, and breathe your business. Your side hustle is your baby, and like all newborns, to thrive it requires round-the-clock attention and nourishment. You also have to have a thick skin. If you are intimidated by the word "no," then you might as well call it a day and go back to your comfortable desk job.

Once we had our inventory and I had set up the website, things quickly began to fall into place. I still remember my first sale. It was from a lady named Emelda. She was Nigerian, funny enough, and she was sending the hair back home to re-sell because she had a store there. It was such a thrill when those first orders came in, but I needed to dedicate all my time to the business or I wouldn't be able to build it. Within a month, we were making enough sales that it made sense for me to quit my job at the bank so I could focus on expanding the business. I had seen other people make a living selling hair extensions, so I had faith I could do it. Finally, I was able to devote all my energy to doing the thing I loved. I thought of my mother and how she always threw herself into her different business ventures, and I understood for the first time where her entrepreneurial drive came from. It was never about the money, it was about the thrill of building and creating; it was about having ownership of your successes and your failures.

We had been working out of our apartment, but as the business grew, we needed somewhere to house our inventory as well as a physical location to sell from. I approached a woman who owned a salon in Duluth, and she agreed to rent me a small space in her shop. I was doing well through the website and the shop, but things really began to take off when I started getting referrals from a local beauty supply store. At the time, brick and mortar wholesalers only carried synthetic hair; extensions made from real human hair that you could bleach, color, and style were radical, and consumers could not get enough. I had a product that was in high demand; I just needed to get the word out. I went to a local beauty supply store and took the sales girl aside. I gave her my card and told her that if a customer came in looking for Brazilian or Indian hair, which was not sold at the beauty supply store at the time, and she referred them to me, I would give her a 10 percent cut of the sale.

Almost immediately, she started sending me referrals. Hair was sold in bundles priced at fifty dollars. Most customers needed at least three bundles to get the look they wanted, so we were averaging one hundred and fifty dollars per sale, and a wholesale order could be as much as twenty-five hundred dollars per order. We quickly got to the point where we were bringing in enough money to pay rent *and* take care of the business. Within three months, we were getting so many orders it got to be too much for me to manage on my own.

One day I went to pick Mansour up from work, and when he saw how exhausted I was, we realized that for the business to keep growing at this pace, we both needed to focus our time. We rolled the dice again, and he quit his job so we could both focus on running the business full time. Drawing on our individual skill sets, I focused on inventory and customer service, while Mansour focused on logistics and order fulfillment. It was divide and conquer.

With more time to focus on streamlining the business, I started experimenting with our inventory and testing different markets for distributors. Initially, all our hair came from India, but then we heard that the hair coming out of China had improved. At first no one trusted China because the concern was it would be inferior quality. You might think *hair is hair*, but processing techniques are essential to the strength and quality of the end product. The chemicals needed to sanitize and strip away the original color and to produce different curl patterns and colors are very strong and can affect the integrity of the hair depending on the method used. When a higher quality of chemicals and a more artful approach to processing is used, the result is higher quality product. When I heard that the hair coming out of China was just as good as hair that was being sold from India or Brazil, I decided to give it a try. Customers didn't notice the difference. That was when we realized that all the big companies were actually selling Chinese hair. Everyone denied it and pretended that they didn't buy hair from China, but the reality was that Chinese distributors supplied a competent product for half the price, and they shipped in two days, where India could take two weeks. Overnight, we were able reduce our inventory cost, improve our shipping time, and widen our profit margin.

Just when it seemed like everything was falling into place, the woman who owned the salon where I was renting space saw how well the business was doing and decided she wanted a piece of the action. She wanted a partnership, but I wasn't interested. From day one, I never wanted a partner. If it wasn't my husband, I was not interested. Unfortunately, she knew the girl who was referring customers to me, and I believe she turned her against me, because as soon as I turned her down, the referrals dried up. I realized too late that we had been relying so heavily on these referrals that without them the business wasn't generating enough revenue to support itself. We had invested everything we had in the business and Mansour had left his job, so we had no other source of income. We were so broke we had to borrow money just to pay our utilities. We had no food in the fridge and no money for rent. It was truly rock bottom. We had risked everything, and now we had nothing to show for it, less than nothing.

There was a huge part of me that felt so defeated I considered giving up, but then I decided I wasn't going down without a fight. I had been hearing about a new social media platform, and I decided to give it a try. Back then, we had no clue about Instagram, how people communicated with one another, or why they were posting photos. I jumped back into research mode. We looked at other pages and learned how to search for businesses like ours. We noticed some of them had ten or twenty thousand followers. They were posting photos of their hair extensions, with captions and hashtags. We studied their customers, their pricing structure, and their business models. We learned that other users could comment under your photos and that you could respond. Suddenly we had a direct line to our consumer base.

This was the early days of social media advertising, and it was a revolutionary frontier for small businesses. This little icon on your phone changed the landscape of marketing and advertising for thousands of small businesses. It leveled the playing field and opened a whole new world for us, allowing us to establish a strong presence and build a large audience of potential customers. We quickly built a following and established our brand in the marketplace. With the referrals from the beauty salon, we were getting one or two sales a week; once we started advertising on Instagram, that jumped to six sales a day, and then it jumped to eleven sales, then to twenty. We encouraged our customers to post photos and shout us out if they liked our product, and then we would repost those photos on our account. The more people shouted us out, the more orders we got. The more orders we got, the more photos we were able to repost. The more photos we reposted, the more trust we built. The more trust we built, the more orders we got. And so on, and so on.

Sometimes opportunities come disguised as obstacles. If those referrals hadn't dried up, I never would have tried something so radically new. I do believe things happen for a reason. In life, and in business, you have to be prepared for the unexpected and dig deep to find the strength to see your way through it. In the space of little more than a year, I had changed my course in life and met the love of my life; I had experienced the euphoric highs of success and the devastating lows of failure. Along the way, I was learning valuable lessons about life, love, and business that made me stronger and wiser. I was on an exhilarating path, and I couldn't wait to find out what lay around the next corner.

CHAPTER 7

THE MOTHER OF (RE)INVENTION

I 've read that the number of female-owned businesses grew by 74 percent between 1997 and 2015. That's one and a half times the national average. As I write this, women now own 30 percent of all businesses in the U.S., and women of color control 14 percent of those; that's roughly 1.3 million businesses. I am one of those women, and I kid you not, my success is all down to the fact that I learned very early on how to use social media as a marketing tool. The internet is the great equalizer. There are no walls and no glass ceilings, only a wide-open field of commerce and fair trade.

Instagram was a dream come true for small business owners. In less than a decade after it launched, it now has its own culture, with over five hundred million active users (and counting) sharing images on the app every single day.

It has become a global community of artisans, entertainers, manufacturers, consumers, celebrities, and tastemakers that exists at the intersection where commerce and culture meet. Instagram is where you go to find unique items that are tailored specifically to your interests and style. It could be hats, swimsuits, subscription boxes, artisanal cheeses, eyelashes—you name it, you will find it on Instagram. All the big guys—the Macy's, the Kohl's—have monopolized the brick and mortar retail market, but they've lost touch with smaller businesses and emerging market trends. Everything in the mall is mass-produced; by the time you see a holographic backpack or unicorn onesie at Nordstrom, that product has already reached market saturation, and more often than not, its cultural relevance has peaked. There are products on Instagram you will never find at the big retail chains, and that is why the malls are dying.

Instagram came on the scene, and suddenly millions of small businesses had a global platform. It became a marketplace for all of us. Small business owners were the ones who recognized that it was such an effective marketing tool—at the time, even Instagram didn't understand its own potential. The beauty of Instagram is the fact that you can do just about anything in terms of imagery: lush photos of your product, videos, memes, motivational quotes, anything that will catch the consumer's eye and attract attention to your business. We were able to market our products directly to consumers, who in turn got specifically what they wanted. Small business owners were becoming millionaires underground, and we were doing it all through this little icon on our phones. These days it's hard to imagine any kind of marketing strategy that doesn't involve social media, but when we started out, it was totally uncharted territory. I was able to build and grow my business without much capital up front, and once I got the taste for it, I was determined to build an empire.

To be honest, when I first started out, I didn't want my face out front. I was worried I might be too young or that mainstream America might not embrace an African business owner. I wanted people to feel comfortable with my brand, and I was concerned they might think I was not embedded in the culture and therefore may not trust my offerings. I hired people who were relatable and for whom there wasn't a language barrier. I felt I needed to build the brand first, so as not to be misunderstood or marginalized into a niche category. The bottom line is, whatever obstacle came in the way of me making money, I was going to remove it. In the beginning I was very cautious, but as I grew more confident as a business owner, I realized that for the sake of the company, I needed to be out front as the face of our brand.

The beauty of the internet is that anyone can throw his or her hat into the ring. All you need is ambition, a little bit of capital, and a dream. When we started selling hair extensions, I was able to get a domain name and a fully functional website for nine dollars a month. By tapping into online outsourcing services (like Fiverr, Elance, and Freelancer), we were able to create infrastructure and establish brand identity, without compromising competitive pricing. We outsourced everything from graphic designers to customer service reps, which allowed us the opportunity to look professional without breaking the bank. Our first hire was a customer service rep in the Philippines who helped me handle customer inquiries and take orders over the phone. We created an account for her to be able to access our website on the backend and trained her through Skype and shared screens on how to process orders, navigate the website, and get answers from our

FAQ page. Since the calls were recorded, I was able to monitor her work, even though she was thirteen hours ahead and nine thousand miles away.

Outsourcing is definitely a mixed bag. Just because someone is charging less doesn't mean they know what they are doing or that they can do it well. A customer service rep that does not communicate properly can negatively impact your business. If a rep is talking too fast, too slow, or not clearly enough, you can lose customers out of frustration. As we took on more freelancers, I noticed one of our reps was reliable, but she was robotic and wasn't catching on to cultural cues. She would always repeat what the customers said when they called with a problem and they would often get impatient and hang up. Another issue we had with freelancers was that they would take on more jobs than they were supposed to. Calls would be coming in, but they weren't getting answered, which in retail is absolutely unacceptable.

As our business began to grow, so did our family. In August of 2013, I gave birth to our first son. We named him Obi, the Igbo word for *heart*. At that point, I was still going to school part time and running the business full time. I was one credit short of my associates' degree in accounting and had been accepted to Georgia State University. The plan was to finish out the semester and begin taking classes toward my bachelor's degree in the spring. Little did I know the business was about to take a whole new direction that would change the course of our lives forever.

Within two years of launching the website, we had mastered Instagram marketing and established a recognizable and popular brand in the marketplace. We were making daily visits to the post office to fulfill our orders and ship our product out to our customers. We thought we were at the top of our game and were generally feeling impressed with the success of our little ecommerce business. Then one day Mansour came home from sending off a shipment of orders. He was all excited because he had been standing in line next to a woman who he estimated was shipping out three or four times more product than we were. She had a huge orange cart, the biggest one they had at the post office, full of packages. When one fell out of the cart and onto the floor, Mansour bent down to help her pick it up, cleverly taking note of the name of her company on the shipping label. We immediately looked her up on Instagram, and it turned out she was selling a type of body-shaping product called a "waist trainer" or "waist cincher," which is a corset-like belt designed to flatten the belly and slenderize the waist. With twenty thousand followers on her Instagram page, we realized this woman had tapped into a booming market. The light bulb went off, and I said to myself, "I want in!"

The concept of "body shaping" has existed for centuries and is practiced in many cultures all over the world. In Nigeria after a mother gives birth, the women in her community will tie her belly with a long, brightly patterned cloth, and she will wear that wrapper for several months to squeeze out excess fluids and help her get back to her pre-mommy body. In South America, where there is a popular culture of corseting, Colombian and Brazilian women call them *faja,* from the Spanish word for wrap. In the United States, doctors will recommend the use of abdominal "binders" after a C-section or other abdominal surgery to reduce swelling, pain, and soreness in the stomach muscles.

Funnily enough, this was a product I had been using myself for years. First, to mold my figure into that ideal hour-glass shape when going out to the club, and then later, after giving birth to my son, as a noninvasive way to get my *snap* back. However, even though I was an avid consumer of this product, up until that moment I hadn't considered its market potential. From my own experience, I knew the best cinchers were made in Colombia, where the workmanship was always meticulous. I went straight to Google and began researching manufacturers. Before long, I found myself on a Colombian website buying my first shipment of cinchers.

We already knew what type of platform to use, how to have a website set up for marketing and selling a product, how to create customer service channels, like a toll free number and LiveChat, and where to get reps. I set up a website and an Instagram page. For the website, we used the URL 1800Cinchers.com. We wanted a name that would be very simple and easy to search, like 1-800-Flowers, as well as give our customers a feeling of familiarity and trust. Many of our customers would be women who were using cinchers for a targeted workout and new moms looking to get back into the shape they were in before giving birth, so for our Instagram page we chose the username @slimgirlshapewear to position ourselves as a lifestyle brand that promoted healthy living through shapewear and exercise. We were immediately successful. Our first shipment of waist cinchers sold out within two weeks. I was definitely a pro at marketing and selling online at this point. We applied the same infrastructure and marketing strategies we had used with our hair extension business to the cinchers, and it was more successful because a) we were more seasoned, and b) it was an emerging trend.

Once I saw how well we were doing with the cinchers, I did not think twice about quitting hair. I didn't even finish selling the inventory we had in stock; we just fulfilled all the remaining orders and closed down the website and Instagram page.

Even though we were technically a new company, I decided we didn't need to come across like one. I felt it was important not to give the impression that we were less experienced than we were. When we first started the GoDaddy account, our order numbers started from 0001. Then it occurred to me that nobody wants to be your trial and error. So I changed it so that our numbers began at a more random number, like 8045. Perception is a powerful tool, and I didn't want anyone to feel like they were the first customer, or even tenth.

We weren't afraid to pivot, and the timing could not have been better for us. We were at a stage in our growth as a business where we were seasoned and experienced, but not so invested that we couldn't restructure and reinvent ourselves. At that point, the retail market for hair was becoming saturated, but with cinchers, we were coming in on the ground floor with a product that was ahead of the curve. You'd be surprised how much business owners control market trends. The vast majority of the time when a product becomes a phenomenon, it's not random. Nothing happens overnight. It may seem like a product is suddenly everywhere, but it usually happens with a single or small group of businesses using targeted strategies to bring a product into focus in the market. And in the age of social media, it almost never looks like an advertisement because ads turn people off. When something is new, you have about a year to enjoy it before you hit market saturation. It's a frenzy, and the pioneers will make millions. This economy is that powerful.

The natural success of the cinchers inspired me to go deeper and try newer and better social media marketing strategies. That was when I discovered the power of influencer marketing. I was very much aware that retailers were using high profile individuals to promote their products on social media. I'd see my favorite reality TV celebrities promoting something on their Instagram pages, and I'd wonder how that company got their product into his or her hands. I was curious, but I assumed it was out of my reach, that these businesses were bigger or had better connections. Then one day I was checking out the page of a reality TV star who was popular at the time, and I noticed that she had her contact information listed in her bio. It had never occurred to me that it might be as simple as sending an email, but I suddenly thought, *Why not?*

Everything in this life is about survival. Yes, you believe in your product and you want to feel noble, but if you cannot market it well, no one will pay attention. It's empty if no one is buying. To survive as a small business owner, you have to be bold and seize every opportunity possible. With that in mind, I contacted this woman saying I would love to advertise with her, and could she please advise on pricing? I was absolutely shocked when she responded within an hour with her preferred size and her terms for promoting our product on her social media platforms. I was through the roof with excitement. We shipped out to her right away, and a few days later she posted a photo wearing our cincher, tagging us in the comment and linking to our website. Now, not only did all of her followers know who we were, they could follow the tag to buy our cinchers directly from us. It was a targeted strategy, and it had an immediate and dramatic impact on our sales. Literally overnight, our orders increased by 300 percent. In fact, the spike was so huge that we actually got a "friendly" call from PayPal looking to verify that we were a real company. It was bananas.

Orders were coming in faster than we could fill them. At the time, we were buying directly from Colombia in small batches, and we couldn't keep up with the sudden demand. The way I see it, if I'm out of stock, I'm losing money. I never want to sell out of a product because being sold out means no money is coming in. My business philosophy has always come down to four core rules:

Never let a customer query go unanswered.
Never miss any opportunity to close a sale.
Ship every order within twenty-four hours.
Never go out of stock.

I am always working to ensure the website or our business model makes it easy to make a sale. If something is getting in the way of me being able to sell my product, my mission becomes to eliminate that obstacle. Making that sale is my number one goal. What stands in the way of making that sale has to go or be adjusted.

And what was standing in my way at that point was getting my hands on enough product quickly enough to fill all the orders we had coming in. It could take anywhere from thirty to sixty days to import our cinchers from the manufacturer in Colombia. I had to find a local source where I could buy in larger volume. Thankfully, I found a distributor in Duluth who had been in the game longer than we had and was buying the same cinchers from Colombia in bulk. I was able to order directly from him to meet the demand in sales. We had to pay twice the price for the same product, but in return I was able to increase the volume and speed of my supply. I'd rather make ten dollars less on five hundred orders, than ten dollars more on three or five orders. I didn't mind buying from this local distributor if it meant he would provide me with what I needed right away, as opposed to having to wait three weeks for the product to ship from Columbia. Mind you, I was still ordering from Colombia because I was getting it at the same price he was. Soon we were placing orders of ten thousand and twenty thousand dollars. I remember this distributor asking me at the end of that year, "Do you realize you've purchased almost a million dollars' worth of product?" And it all started from influencer marketing. It was so innocent at the time, so new and so fresh.

Reality TV celebrities like the Housewives and the Kardashians have become a driving force of the marketplace. Women want to dress like them and aspire to their lifestyle. Working with these kinds of influencers allowed me the opportunity to put my product in front of millions of people for 1 percent of what it would have cost to advertise on a television network. Once I had success with one celebrity, I started reaching out to other influencers. It became a snowball effect. Because of the success we had with these influencers, we were now moving in circles where we were meeting people who could help us with branding. I met with a publicist who represented one of the women I wanted to promote our product, and she asked me if we had a publicist, which of course we didn't at the time. She explained she didn't just work with celebrities, she also worked with companies to build and promote their brand identities through social media. I hired her, and she gave us way more exposure than we ever thought possible on our own.

Slim Girl Shapewear had taken off so quickly that I made the very difficult decision to put school on hold indefinitely so I could focus on building the business. I had an infant son and an infant business to nurture, and they both needed my attention to thrive and flourish. To this day, I am conflicted about not finishing my degree. Education has always been important to me, as it had been to my father, but this dream of being an entrepreneur burned so fiercely within me I couldn't divide my attention any longer.

We had started out with simple black latex cinchers, but the consumer appetite for variety was insatiable. Manufacturers had begun introducing workout cinchers, which came in different colors and prints. They had the same function, but people wanted them customized to fit their preferences. Whether it was bright pink or leopard print, our customers wanted to be able to work out in a cincher that reflected their individual personalities. We branched out from the classic black latex cincher and began carrying them in a rainbow of colors and prints. We also had customers that were allergic to latex, and we worked with our manufacturer in Colombia on a prototype for a non-latex cincher. I had samples made in my size so I could test them out on myself. We went back and forth with the manufacturer, trying out different kinds of materials that didn't contain latex but that would still be strong and stretchy enough to have the firm hold of the traditional cincher. In the end, we settled on a material called Powernet, a cotton-based fabric used in post-surgical garments. All of a sudden, people who couldn't use latex now had access to a well-made and functional waist cincher. The non-latex cincher was a huge success for us. We could never have enough in stock.

Now that we were immersed in the body-shaping world, we began expanding into other products related to slimming around the midsection. We began carrying a product called Slim Gel, made with green tea and seaweed, which was designed to promote perspiration. You rub it around your belly before a workout and then put a waist cincher on top of it so you sweat more around your midsection. We had customers who wanted to cover back fat, and we began carrying waist cincher vests that were higher on the back area and came over the shoulder. It shaped around the waist and also had back coverage. Our customers wanted that hourglass shape—big butt, tiny waist. We took it a step further than the waist cinchers by adding Butt Lifters to our product inventory. These were waist-shaping shorts made out of cotton with cutouts around the butt and latex around the waist area for that restricted, firm hold. We carried all these products in a variety of colors and prints, in latex and non-latex, and in sizes going from XS all the way up to 7XL.

Up to now, we had been working out of our home. At this point, we had so much inventory it was becoming impossible for Mansour and I to process all of the orders ourselves. The woman I hired to help me take care of Obi began helping out as my personal assistant, but we needed more staff. I contacted a temp agency about hiring extra workers to help us process orders, but we found out they wouldn't send temps to a residential office. It was clear we now needed a dedicated base of operations.

I was aware that a lot of our customers struggled with sizing. Being someone who's always looking for a solution as a way to gain competitive advantage, I decided our new headquarters could also double as a storefront. We would have space to house all of our inventory *and* our local customers would be able to come to the store to get fitted properly. We found a 1,500 square-foot retail space in Duluth and moved our inventory out of our home. We used half the space for the store and half the space for our online office and processing department.

With the help of our new publicist, we mounted a huge marketing campaign for our grand opening. We had two billboards advertising the opening and paid for ad time on a local radio station. We hired a reality TV celebrity to come do a meet-and-greet, and she promoted the opening through her social media. All the advertising paid off. The grand opening of our Slim Girl Shapewear store was a huge success. So many people came out that day, we were filled to capacity. We had people lining up outside waiting to come in.

A lot of opportunities came from having a commercial location. We were able to apply for business accounts and set up shipping accounts. To tell you how successful we got, while we were prepping for the grand opening, Mansour and I saw the cincher lady from the post office hanging around out front. She must have heard about us because of the buzz we were creating and was obviously passing by to check us out. She knew she was the It Girl in shapewear, and she wanted to find out who these upstarts were that were luring all her customers away. By then, she had already blocked us on Instagram, but we had made enough noise that she was actually curious enough to come down and check us out in person. It was so surreal that Mansour and I both happened to be there to see her. I will never forget that moment because that was when I *knew* we had made it.

CHAPTER 8

THE WENDY FRENZY

W ithin a year of opening the store, we grew to the point where we needed a separate dedicated headquarters for the online business. We moved out of the store and into a five thousand-square-foot warehouse in Duluth. Although online sales accounted for the bulk of our revenue, we decided to keep the physical store open so local customers could continue to come in to get sized. It was a thrill to be in our new location. For a year, we had been crammed into half of the 1,500-square-foot retail space, but now that we had moved into the warehouse, we had space for our online inventory, a dedicated shipping department, a call center, and separate offices for Mansour and myself.

We were now a much bigger and more streamlined operation. I was enjoying the high of being big and successful, and I was hungry for more. Determined to build my empire, I didn't stop to take a break or even a breath. I was just going, going, going! I never paused to consider *how* I was growing the business or *where* I wanted to go with it. There are some lessons in life you can only learn from experience, and for me, the pitfalls of rapid growth turned out to be one of those lessons.

Up to now, we had been relying solely on influencer marketing. It was time to spread our wings and try different platforms. We hired influential bloggers to review our cinchers and drive consumer attention to our website. We also branched into print ads, publishing in magazines like *Stars, Ok, Self,* and *Health.* I didn't really see much return investment in terms of sales, but it helped our credibility and made us look good.

Next, we set our sights on getting our cinchers on TV. We reached out to a few daytime chat shows and heard back almost immediately from *The Wendy Williams Show,* who were interested in doing a feature on our cinchers. We flew to New York and met with her team to discuss pricing and terms. The deal included a fifty-dollar gift card for each member of her studio audience to purchase the waist cincher of her choice and size from our website and a 20 percent off call-to-action coupon code for her viewers. It was agreed she would run a two-minute segment on waist cinchers, which featured 1800cinchers.com. As key as the internet is in terms of marketing, the next natural step for us was television. It's kind of like how celebrities always want to have a book deal. It gives them legitimacy and elevates the brand. If you have a product, you want to be endorsed on television. It's about sales, but it's also about establishing credibility and brand recognition. The credibility you can get from a show like *Wendy Williams* is worth the investment.

At ten o'clock on the morning of the appointed day, we had our shipping department and our customer service reps standing by ready to take orders. We thought we were ready. We thought we were big enough to handle *Wendy.* The truth is we had no idea what we were getting ourselves into. Within minutes of the segment airing, the phones in our call center were ringing off the hook. No sooner had our reps finished with one call when another was coming in. People were reaching out on social media because they had heard about us on the show and wanted to shout us out or learn more about our products. When I took a look at our sales chart at the end of the day, I could barely believe my eyes. It was bananas.

Out of stock in our most popular items, we went to the local distributor in Duluth and replenished whatever we could on the website. The next day, the new inventory was gone in an hour. This kept happening day after day. People were buying whatever we had available. We took what we could from the store, but after a while, all we had left were off-sizes and unpopular colors, like extra small and nude. When the distributor in Duluth ran dry, I literally started buying from competitors just to keep things in stock. No one could supply me with the inventory I needed as quickly as I needed it, and I had no choice but to zero out products on the website. Given that one of my core business principles was to never sell out, this was absolutely unacceptable to me. I had invested in this incredibly successful advertisement, and now I wasn't getting my full money potential because I didn't have enough product to sell.

It was such a rush having so many customers clamoring to buy our body-shaping products. But as much as it was a blessing to be selling so much, it ended up becoming a complete disaster because we weren't ready for it. Within days, we had so little inventory left that many of the audience members who had received gift cards couldn't find anything to buy, and we had nothing to offer customers who needed to make an exchange. I had ten reps manning the phones, but it wasn't enough. While we were doing our best, customers felt like we weren't because we couldn't handle the volume of calls coming in. We were not prepared at all. Then the social media backlash came. We started getting bad reviews and complaints online about our customer service. Even though we were answering customer queries within twenty-four hours, they were frustrated they weren't getting a response after an hour or two.

In the middle of this madness, someone in the shipping department, I never found out who, mistakenly duplicated about five hundred orders. Once we caught the mistake, we began the tedious process of separating out the duplicate orders, but in the meantime, hundreds of customers were receiving two shipments of the same product. We didn't have enough inventory to fulfill the orders we had, and now we were over here dealing with duplicate orders. It was just a mess. Such a rookie mistake. We had bitten off way more than we could chew, and we ended up suffering from it for months.

If I'd had ten thousand pieces at the time, I probably could have sold all of them. The demand was that high. I increased production, because I definitely did not enjoy losing customers. While all this was going on, I was also trying to scale; a business that scales well should be able to maintain the quality of its product and its level of efficiency when tested by larger operational demand. A big part of that process is to find ways to reduce the cost of manufacturing your product as you increase your level of production. The market is so competitive. Competition with the Chinese is fierce. American retailers and manufacturers have higher overhead and more expenses, but we have to stay competitive. The only way to do that is to keep the price of your product low. If I was getting a product wholesale for sixteen dollars per piece, I wanted to be able to buy it for fourteen dollars. A difference of just two dollars per item could translate to ten thousand dollars in savings for the volume I was buying.

Even fifty cents an item was a huge savings. What I saved, I immediately reinvested in our inventory and overhead to scale the business.

We were zeroed out on everything, with orders pending. I rushed to order in bulk from a new manufacturer in Colombia because I was desperate to keep up with the demand. The frenzy was already starting to die down a little bit, but I was still on a high. I thought the customers who hadn't been able to buy from us would be waiting for me to replenish, and when I did, they would come back. I placed a huge volume of orders. That was a big mistake, and it ended up coming back to haunt me. At first, I was ecstatic when our new shipment of cinchers finally came in and we could start shipping them out to customers. But almost immediately, we started getting calls from our customers about receiving defective waist trainers. At this point, it was a month after Wendy had aired her segment, so we were much more visible as a brand and therefore a bigger and more vulnerable target. Our cinchers are super sturdy and well made, so I couldn't understand the complaints that were coming in. We were like, "What are they talking about?" Mansour pulled a few of the cinchers from the warehouse, and when he applied pressure to them, to our absolute horror, we discovered that the front hooks were glued on instead of sewn in. On top of that, the sizing was off. We decided to pull the rest of the stock from the manufacturer in Colombia, and of the six thousand pieces we had ordered, 80 percent of them were defective.

When we called the manufacturer to find out what had happened, his excuse was that he had outsourced production to another company, and they were the ones that had manufactured the defective cinchers. He also sold his own line of cinchers and sent us videos and photos of his own returned defective merchandise. Clearly, his brand was having the same issues we were having. That was how we figured out he *knew* about the defects but never told us they sent us a bad batch. Foolishly, he thought I wouldn't notice he had mixed the defective cinchers into our shipment. Never mind the customers, never mind my credibility. We were shipping out products to customers thinking we were sending out the same quality as always, and I was totally blindsided by the customer backlash. To try and regain our trust, he flew us out to Colombia so we could tour his factory. He merged his line with ours and designated a section of the factory to producing our cinchers. He refunded the orders that were defective and bit by bit sent us corrections. Eventually, I found another Colombian manufacturer who could supply me with a better-quality product for an even cheaper price, so I was able to cut ties with him. Still, the damage was done. We had passed the peak sales bump we'd gotten from *The Wendy Williams Show*, and now we were dealing with the opposite issue of overstock. To this day, I have inventory from that order that I am still trying to sell.

When we weren't able to fulfill orders, we were losing theoretical money, but now we were dealing with products being returned, and that meant we were now losing actual money. We had invested hundreds of thousands of dollars in this shipment and tied up liquid cash that I could have reinvested in the business or simply saved for my family. But more than the financial loss, what devastated me the most was the damage to our reputation. I had worked so hard to build customer trust, and now we were losing new customers, repeat customers, and potential repeat customers. It was a lot of damage control. For a six-month period, we were quenching one fire or another.

Then, just as we were beginning to right the ship, waist cinchers suddenly became a controversial product. After Wendy introduced the body-shaping industry to the mainstream, there was a frenzy among online retailers to be "The" shapewear brand. We were all trying to one up each other. Then we heard, "Oh my God. Have you seen Kim? She's wearing a waist cincher!" And that was it. Once the Kardashians started advertising them, waist cinchers captivated not only the attention of consumers, the entire industry was exposed to the glaring eye of the media. Suddenly, "celebrity" doctors were coming out of the woodwork, denouncing waist cinchers as dangerous and unhealthy on their TV shows. A lot of these same doctors were promoting weight loss pills and plastic surgery, but because we did not pay homage to them, they went on the attack. The truth is, they were riding the popularity of waist cinchers in their own way, tapping into the trend and capitalizing on the public's fascination. Even the almighty Dr. Oz decided to come out against the waist cincher industry.

To this day, it's difficult to advertise waist cinchers. Some platforms will charge double because cinchers are considered as controversial as a weight loss pill. However, despite the controversy, the industry has survived and thrived because of consumer loyalty. We support and celebrate the female body in all its shapes, colors, and sizes. All we were trying to do was simply help women to achieve the shape they want and feel good about their bodies. Our brand promotes a healthy approach to beauty and encourages women to embrace their curves. The accusations against the industry were sensationalized by so-called "celebrity" doctors who stood to benefit from the controversy by a boost in ratings. The truth is, many of our customers who had been considering having tummy tucks or liposuction, both procedures that come with far greater risk of danger the any body-shaping product, decided not to go through with it because of our waist cinchers.

Sometimes growth is relative. You definitely do not want to grow too fast. I'll never forget a piece of advice I got from a manufacturer I met with when I went to New York in advance of the *Wendy Williams Show*. When I told him that I wanted to sell my brand at Wal-Mart, he asked me, "Do you think you're ready?" When I told him I thought I was, he warned me that he had seen a lot of small businesses go bankrupt selling to Wal-Mart. At the time I thought, *Oh, please. It cannot be that hard. We can handle it.* But the fact is, we could not even handle Wendy. What I learned later is that big chains like Wal-Mart require a certain volume in production. What often happens is that small companies will take a loan and invest all the capital they have to keep up with production. Then if something goes wrong, if the order isn't complete or you miss a deadline or a procedure, Wal-Mart will reject the whole order, driving that business into bankruptcy.

Rapid growth isn't always the right path. This is the cautionary tale of what happens when you get too big too fast and you don't have the inventory or the structure to keep up with a sudden increase in sales. All the time I was having success, we were making money, but I wasn't sleeping or eating. It became a tsunami of issues, and I was dealing with one crisis after another. I didn't have time for my family. I was a complete zombie. All I could do was deal with each issue one step at a time, one day at a time.

There are times you face challenges like that and you think it will never stop. For six solid months, it was just back-to-back crises, but we found our way through it. Running a small business is not an easy road to walk. We tapped into this incredible market and had a lot of success in a short amount of time, but there's no fairytale ending. True success requires constant hard work, every moment of every day.

CHAPTER 9

THE REAL DEAL

For the first three years after we started the shapewear business, I barely slept. In that short amount of time, we had gone from processing orders out of our apartment to having a retail location and an online headquarters. Although being featured on *The Wendy Williams Show* catapulted us to a new level of success, I was so focused on trying to fulfill the orders we had in front of us that I didn't get to enjoy it at all. I also had a newborn son who I adored and who was the light in my life, but I was missing out on precious moments because I was always working and worrying about the company. Between the online business, the retail store, motherhood, and managing one crisis after another, I was stretched too thin.

It was time to prioritize.

It had been two years since we opened the store. Although sales were steady enough that it was paying for itself, 90 percent of our income was generated from the online business. Amazon normalized online shopping, so consumers were no longer hesitant to buy from retail websites. I saw the writing on the wall and realized that it made more sense to channel our resources into expanding our brand and continuing to build the online business. Managing the store required more focus than I was willing to give, so we decided to let the lease run out and close it down.

With a little bit more room to breathe and time to think, I began dreaming and planning what our next move would be. It's one thing to run a company with a single product, but once your business begins to scale, you need product and brand extensions. You need to stay fresh and give your customers incentive to keep buying from you over your competitors. At the time waist cinchers were a trend, and the thing about trends is that they burn fierce and then they fade out. For a brand to thrive in the marketplace, it has to evolve and grow. If we were to survive beyond the trend, we needed to set ourselves apart from our competitors and expand our brand.

When it came time to decide what our next product would be, I worked closely with our customer service team who were on the front lines, fielding customers' queries and complaints. Over the years, as we have grown and added new products, it was always based on the feedback we were getting from customers. I am always tweaking, adding, switching, and adjusting according to consumer interest. To this day, I hear every single complaint and every bit of feedback we get from our customers.

From the beginning, we had a lot of customers who would go to the gym and then post selfies working out in our cinchers. The idea is to put pressure and heat on the midsection to train the muscles and provide a more targeted workout. As waist trainers became more and more popular, we were getting consistent feedback that our customers wanted a more diverse line of shapewear that they could wear to the gym. They wanted something that was functional but which would also be less visible and cumbersome than a traditional waist cincher. So we began working on designs for shapewear leggings that would be both fashionable and functional. I sent sketches of my vision to our manufacturer in Colombia, who sent back samples in my size based on my designs. For anything that I'm making, I always use myself as the model so I can judge the fit and quality of the construction. After some trial and error, we came up with our signature Cinch Leggings. The latex-reinforced waist came up to just below the bust and provided that firm hold around the abdomen our customers were looking for, without the need to wear a separate cincher. We had them made in capri and full length, as well as a non-latex version.

The launch of our Cinch Leggings was a success, but what really put us over the top was that we got Khloé Kardashian to endorse them on her social media. She posted a stunning photo of herself wearing our Cinch Leggings, looking every inch the voluptuous goddess, with the caption, "Ladies, these babies will suck you in and make curves look seriously amazing." That post, which tagged Slim Girl Shapewear and directed customers to our website, was picked up by fitness and fashion blogs all over the internet. The Kardashians are the queens of influencer marketing, so it was a coup to have Khloé endorse our new line of Cinch Leggings. Even our competitors were reaching out to congratulate us. For weeks, we were basking in the Kardashian glow. Wendy introduced our waist cinchers to the mainstream, but Khloé made our Cinch Leggings look sexy and cool. The attention we got from that one simple post broadened our platform and expanded our reach as a brand.

After the success of the Khloé post, I wanted to strike while the iron was still hot and capitalize on the buzz of our launch. And if truth be told, I was still chasing that high I had felt after the frenzy from *The Wendy Williams Show*. About a month after the launch, we reached out to *The Real* and made a deal with them to feature our Cinch Leggings on their show. With its young hosts and youthful demographic, I was hoping to reach the same consumer base that had been so excited by the Khloé post. To their credit, *The Real* team came up with a great concept. They approached the segment with a sense of humor and did a spoof of the infomercial format. They brought out two beautiful, full-figured models, one wearing regular leggings and the other in our Cinch Leggings, so viewers could see for themselves the dramatic shaping effect they would get from our new product. They displayed our different styles and gave out a call-to-action code for 10 percent off the leggings on our website. The segment was fun and energetic, just like the women we were hoping to market to.

This time we were ready. We had ample inventory in our warehouse and a full customer service team poised to take on the floods of orders we anticipated would be coming in. *The Real* segment aired and…nothing. The calls didn't come. They offered to air the segment again two weeks later. Still, the calls didn't come. In the weeks and months that followed, the leggings sold consistently, but it was nowhere near the volume needed to justify the money we had invested in marketing with *The Real*. In assessing where it went wrong, I realized that the failure was the result of two factors: 1) the Cinch Leggings were not as big a trend as the waist cinchers; and 2) *The Real* simply did not have the reach that Wendy had. What I learned from that experience was that every marketing strategy has to be tailor made to fit the product you are looking to promote. You can't have a one-size-fits-all strategy because each product has its own specific market potential. We paid a lot of money for *The Real* segment, and we truly thought it was going to be a huge success, but it was a total flop.

It's good to take risks. I love taking risks. I love the rush that comes with rolling the dice and winning big. However, at the same time you have to be prepared to take a loss. With *The Real,* we took a huge loss. After dealing with all the inventory issues we had following *The Wendy Williams Show,* I had overcompensated with *The Real.* My mistake was that I was just buying and buying and advertising and advertising. I kept putting money right back into the business, trying to get bigger and bigger, that would have been liquid cash for me to save and enjoy. I had lost sight of the bigger picture.

The failure of *The Real* knocked me off my feet. It was a huge blow financially, but more than that, it woke me up to the fact that I'm not invincible. Even with all the setbacks we had struggled through, up to that moment I hadn't truly absorbed the lessons of those experiences. Even in times of success, it's essential that you slow down. You have to learn how to calculate trends and how to calculate inventory. You have to know when to replenish and when to allow a product to zero out. It's critical that you understand customer character. In the twenty-first century, consumers have instant access to infinite retail options. When they have the hunger for a product, if they can't get it from you, they are going to go buy it somewhere else. You can't hold out or expect them to wait because your competitors are just one click away. I love shopping online. Everything I have in my house I bought online. My furniture, my bed, my pots and pans, baby food, baby bottles. I am the typical online consumer, and convenience is just as important to me as it is to everyone else. If you don't have what I want, I will go somewhere else to buy it. It's all about convenience. Customers love convenience, and if you cannot provide it, they'll move on in a heartbeat.

I'm a lot more careful now. I still take risks, but I'm way more cautious. It took a while, but ultimately, I realized that our success with marketing the waist cinchers didn't happen by luck. It happened because of the trend and the frenzy that was going on at that time. Some products have the frenzy effect, some products don't. However, just because we're not creating a frenzy, that doesn't mean we don't have a sellable product. In terms of long-term sales, the Cinch Leggings have been a success for us, but I should have marketed them differently. I should have taken a slow and steady approach to study its organic reach first. A product's organic reach should be exciting before you invest huge marketing dollars. Never force a product down anyone's throat. It's okay to make money slowly and steadily. It doesn't always have to be a 300 percent spike in sales, but by the same token, you don't invest as much in marketing to support that product.

Managing trends is a huge part of dealing with success. I come across companies all the time who are selling trending products, like fidget spinners or hoverboards, and I feel bad for them because I know they're going to go through exactly what I went through. Your sales will soar because of the trend, but if you're not careful, you will crash. If you are like me and you have a policy of never going out of stock, you will learn the hard way the importance of calculating inventory. I should have been perfectly okay with selling out after *The Wendy Williams Show*. Selling out at the right time is the key to riding the wave of a trending product. To this day, I have funds tied up in inventory because I was doing too much. I had to realign my thinking because I was absolutely naïve. That's why experience is good. You're not going to get by on luck forever. If you experience success too quickly or too soon, life will teach you how to handle it.

CHAPTER 10

#ONLYINLAGOS

I was convinced I would never return to Nigeria after my father was killed. Still, I had tried to go home back when we were still selling hair extensions, but it was a total fail. It had been twelve long years since I had left my home, my family, my Nigeria. Although so much had changed for me in that time, it seemed like too many things back home were the same: the daily power outages, the frustration of sitting in bumper-to-bumper traffic for hours on end, the total lack of internet service.

To be closer to her church, my mom had moved from my childhood home on Lagos Island to a small apartment in a remote neighborhood on the outskirts of the city. After she lost the pure water business, she never got back in the game and didn't have much income other than the money we had been sending home. Staying with her in that apartment, I felt isolated and cut off from the life I had built and everything

I had been working so hard to achieve. At that point in my life, I was still so hungry to make my mark on the world, and being back under my mother's roof, totally dependent on others to get around, felt like a huge step backward to me. I was supposed to stay for a week, but I was so unhappy I found myself on a flight back to Atlanta after only three days. I remember standing on a bridge on my way home from an errand and telling myself I would never come back to this country again.Fast forward two years later. We had moved on from hair to shapewear and had just taken 1800Cinchers and Slim Girl Shapewear to the next level with the success of the segment that had aired on *The Wendy Williams Show*. I had found my partner in life and in business, and we had just celebrated our beautiful son's first birthday. Despite all the complications that had come along with the success of the business, I was more content with my life and excited about my future than I had ever been. At the time, my sister who lives in London was planning a trip home and suggested I join her. I thought, *Maybe...*

But I knew if I went back, it had to be on my own terms. While I was looking into flights, I discovered that I was actually able to search for hotels in Lagos, read reviews from people who had stayed there, and even book a room online. *What?* That was totally new. Then I found out that Uber had launched in Lagos earlier that year. That was a total game changer, because it meant for the first time I would be able to get around the city on my own. The ease of the planning was so surprising that before I knew it I had booked a room at prestigious hotel in Lekki that boasted twenty-four-hour electricity and internet access, *and* purchased airline tickets not just for myself but for my husband and son as well.

One week later, Mansour, Obi, and I were on a plane bound for Murtala Muhammed International Airport. The twelve-hour flight was grueling, especially with a toddler in tow. The whole thing is a blur now. I only remember the crying, the endless walking up and down the aisles to distract Obi and keep him entertained, the anxious feeling growing in the pit of my stomach as our plane drew closer and closer to the continent. I was excited to be introducing my husband and son to the Nigeria that I loved with all my heart, but was I truly ready to be back home?

From the moment we arrived in the city, I was immediately struck by how much things had changed in two years. Lagos had gotten even busier and more advanced. Everyone was computer savvy, and there was reliable access to the internet all over the city. This was big for us because it meant we could stay in touch with the business back in Atlanta and check up on orders. We had access to security cameras on our phones, so we were able to monitor the warehouse and the store. We didn't even tell our employees we were out of the country because we didn't want anyone to slack, and we didn't have to because we were able to run things remotely with ease. From the little bit of research I had done booking our hotel, I expected some of those conveniences would be there, but it was still such a surprise to actually experience it for myself. A big part of it was also that our own circumstances had changed. We could afford stay at a more prestigious hotel and to live in a more convenient environment. I was able to enjoy the city in a way that I could never have before because Lagos is an expensive city. When they list the most expensive cities in the world, Lagos is right up there with New York, Paris, Singapore, and Hong Kong.

In some ways, the sights and sounds of Africa's "Big Apple" were the same as always: the hustle and bustle of the city, the insane traffic jams, the boisterous energy of the people. Big, loud, and in-your-face, Lagos is home to nearly twenty million people, every single one of them with ambition and dreams. It's a packed megacity where the streets are teeming with life and the buzz of innovation. People come from all over the world to do business in Lagos because it is Nigeria's economic nerve center. It has always been a melting pot for other Africans—they come to the city to pursue their dreams, the way I had come to the U.S.—but I was surprised by how much more integrated the city now was. I was seeing a lot more foreign faces mixed in among daily life in the city, driving on the roads and shopping in grocery stores. We always had foreigners in Lagos, but you didn't see them mixed in among the general population because they had their own communities.

One thing I had missed almost as much as I missed my family was Nigerian food. Of course, we have Nigerian restaurants in Atlanta, and when I went to visit my sister in London, I had tried the Nigerian restaurants there as well, but no one abroad can truly capture the flavor of true authentic Nigerian cooking. I had been warned by other Nigerian expats, who'd gotten sick when they returned home from eating without discrimination, not to eat the food from vendors on the road. Nigerian street food is not for the faint of heart—or stomach. But from the moment we arrived in Lagos, I was mesmerized. On every curb, you see vendors standing over makeshift wood or coal fires, roasting fish, plantains, meats, and yams. Lagos is a city full of people on the move, always working to make ends meet, and for Lagosians, as we refer to ourselves, street food is a staple. Everywhere I looked, I saw the most tempting dishes: Boli, kilishi, roasted corn, spicy plantain chips, akara, puff puff. I wanted to eat, and eat I did, anywhere and everywhere. I was so carried away that I did not discriminate. I mean, yes, I got an upset stomach a couple of times, but I just drank some water and went right back for more. My appetite for the foods of my youth was insatiable, and fortunately for me, there are two things you will find on virtually every street in Lagos: churches and restaurants. I did not allow the sun to set on a single day while we there before I had eaten my fill of white rice and ofada stew.

The best part was that this time I was sharing these experiences with my husband. Mansour had been looking forward to seeing what this Nigeria I was always talking about was really like for himself. Even though he had grown up in Ghana and was used to the energy of an African city like Accra, nothing can compare to the frenetic energy and high-octane pace of Lagos. I think he captured it perfectly when he described Lagos as "Accra on steroids." Lagos is a city of extremes—the food, the people, even the cars. Everywhere you go, you see people driving these dilapidated junkers they've patched together with scavenged parts from other cars. In fact, in Lagos we have a name for this kind of car: *Things Fall Apart.* For those of you who are not familiar, this nickname is a nod to the seminal novel by Nigerian author Chinua Achebe that is read in every classroom throughout all of Africa. At the same time, you have extreme wealth alongside extreme poverty. You can be sitting in traffic and you might look to your left and see one of these mix-and-match cars chugging along with its Mazda engine inside the body of a beat-up Toyota, and then look to your right and see a Bugatti, a Rolls Royce, or a Lamborghini, perhaps all three.

These two worlds, the glitter and the grime, collide in Lagos all day every day.

One of the highlights of that trip was the day I took Mansour and Obi to visit my old Secondary School, Aunty Ayo Prep. I gave them a tour of the grounds and the classrooms. It was so entertaining to point out what had changed and what had stayed the same, to watch the students hurrying to class and remember myself as a young girl walking those same hallways. I got such a kick when I recognized the familiar face of the gateman at the entrance to the school. I don't know if he remembered me or not, but as soon as he saw my face, he smiled and said, "Oh, Senior, Senior." I had seen that warm smile every day as a girl, but the funny thing was I realized I never knew his name. We always just called him Baba Five Naira because we used to bribe him with ₦5 to let us through the gate when we wanted to skip classes and go party. I wouldn't be surprised if he was still taking bribes from students sneaking out of school to this day, though he's probably called Baba Five Hundred Naira now.

Every day my senses came alive with the sights, smells, and sounds of the city. We'd wake every morning at dawn to the sound of cocks crowing like church bells through the city. From the moment we stepped out of our hotel, my nostrils would fill with the warm, spicy smell of burning wood coming at us from all directions as the street vendors stoked their fires in preparation for the rush of hungry morning commuters. Everywhere we went, my ears were filled with the chatter of the people on the streets, whose conversations are always carried out at full speed and top volume. At the end of every day, with my heart full of the laughter of family and old friends, we'd return to our hotel as a deep orange sun set over Five Cowries Creek and the twinkling lights of Lekki-Ikoyi bridge reflected in the water below. A calm feeling would wash over me as I remembered the Lagos of my childhood.

I was home.

These were the things my heart had missed, without my even realizing it. For the first time in my life, I was no longer intimidated by this raw, untamed city. No, this time I was fascinated by its contradictions and craziness. This time I was a woman in control of my life and my destiny. This time *I* called the shots, and that was a euphoric feeling. Being an adult in this country where I was once a girl was incredible. I loved being able to say whatever I wanted to say, get whatever I wanted to get, go wherever I wanted to go, and leave whenever I wanted to leave. I loved the feeling of being respected and not being at anyone's mercy.

I was energized by the wild sense of lawlessness in the way that people went about their daily lives. In Lagos, things are not manicured or polished. The police officers take bribes with no shame. All kinds of things happen on the road; there's traffic and hold-ups everywhere you go. People always joke that between the traffic in Lagos and the hundreds of thousands of street traders hawking everything from clothes to household goods, you can leave your house naked and by the time you get to your destination you will be fully clothed with all you need. Lagos is not a city that will make things easy for you. You literally have to use your brain to navigate daily life. You have to find your way…no, *make* your way. It does something to you. Your creativity comes to life. There's an intangible "something" about Lagos that makes it a place where anything and everything is possible.

I was enjoying being home and rekindling my relationship with my brothers and sisters. My mom was super excited to finally meet Mansour and her grandson. It was such a joy to watch Obi playing with his cousins. I had been on my own for so long that I had nearly forgotten how good it felt to be among family. My mother and my siblings had seen the *Wendy Williams* segment, and they were super proud of what I had accomplished. I was talking to one of my sisters about the shapewear market in the U.S., and she remarked to me that there was a huge demand for waist cinchers in Nigeria. A light bulb went off in my head.

What if we brought Slim Girl Shapewear to Nigeria? What if we opened a store in Lagos?!

In the two years since my first homecoming, the whole economy of Nigeria had finally tuned into the internet. Nigeria had grown, and though it retained its wild, untamed spirit, it was also less unorganized and more global thinking. With Google, Uber, and Facebook all expanding their reach across the continent, Africa is the next place for a technology boom. I had been thinking about going global with our brand and was intrigued by the opportunities in Africa, but up to then I didn't see how it would ever be possible. Just getting our product to Lagos seemed like an impossible hurdle. It is prohibitively expensive to ship to Africa, and finding a reliable logistics company was no small undertaking. We had tried shipping things in bulk in the past, and it had gone very wrong. When Mansour's mother had moved back to Africa, we had tried to cargo her belongings from Atlanta to Gambia, and it was a total headache. We ended up having to take the shipping company to court to get her things back.

When I got back to Atlanta, I couldn't get the idea of opening a store in Lagos out of my mind, but it seemed impossible to imagine how I could run a company without being there. When it comes to doing business, Nigeria is another beast altogether. On the other hand, if there was a demand for shapewear in Nigeria, it was only a matter of time before someone would fill that need. If I was the waist cincher queen, shouldn't that someone be me? I couldn't unsee what I had seen: the opportunities, the possibilities, the excitement of a booming marketplace just waiting to be conquered by someone with enough ambition and imagination.

I felt super inspired and decided I would just take it one day at a time. My sister had told me that Nigerian realtors now had listings online. I went on these websites to see what commercial properties were available. In short order, I had gotten in touch with a real estate agent in Lagos who found me a promising commercial space in a thriving upscale shopping area on Lagos Island between Lekki and Victoria Island. I had never done business in Nigeria before, so I was definitely scared of being duped. Nigeria back in the day was a scary place to do business. And here I was, six thousand miles from Lagos, trying to do everything online. I was definitely terrified. I didn't want anyone to run away with my money. When you do business abroad and people know you are from America, they look at you like you're basically a cash cow. So I did my research, learned how to search for credibility, and crosschecked what the realtor was quoting me. It seemed comparable to other listings in the area. I decided to go with my heart and take the risk. I talked to Mansour and we agreed to invest fifty thousand dollars into setting up a store in Lagos. That was our threshold for loss, but in truth, my motivation was purely emotional. Nigeria was home, and I was determined to conquer this beast.

When I decide I want something, my ambition kicks into high gear and I move at lightning speed. I had already spoken to the owner of the storefront and talked about pricing and signing the lease. The only that was left was for me to go and see what the retail space looked like for myself. Two weeks later, I was back in Nigeria. And this time I came to work. I had given myself a month, and I fully intended to have the store open and running before I went back to Atlanta. I met with banks and real estate agents. I was a whirlwind. I had been lucky enough to find someone to help us ship out products to Nigeria. My accountant happened to know of a reputable logistics company that shipped to Nigeria for an affordable price. Before I left Atlanta, I had shipped some things back to Nigeria through them simply to test the waters. Within a week, everything had arrived in Lagos safe and sound. Shipping had been the biggest obstacle standing in my way, and with this issue solved, I was ready to bring Slim Girl Shapewear to Nigeria.

I had found a good realtor and a good location. Now I had the place and I had a price. I wasn't experienced enough yet to know that the rent was inflated, but I was definitely shocked that it was the same as what we had been paying at the store in Atlanta, but for half the space. In Nigeria, you don't pay rent monthly for commercial spaces, you pay yearly. Once I signed the lease, I had to pay a full year up front, but it was worth it to be able to begin putting my plan into action. I gave myself two weeks to get the space into shape before our grand opening. I hired painters, carpenters, and interior designers to help set up the store. Things were moving forward like I needed them to. Of course, being that it was Africa and people do not feel the need to rush or be robotic, there were some, shall we say, "hiccups" along the way. One of the biggest frustrations for me was getting workers to keep to my accelerated schedule. Things move slowly and steadily, and deadlines are not taken seriously. In Nigeria, it's a much different pace of life. If a carpenter tells you he is going to be there at ten o'clock in the morning, you need to assume it's not going to happen. Ten a.m. is going to be three p.m., for sure.

I was super impatient from the get-go, and my family had to bring me back to reality. They were like, "Wait a minute, remember you are in Nigeria now." It didn't help that I had already experienced success as a business owner in the States. I had people at my beck and call in Atlanta, so going into opening the store in Lagos, I expected things to be the same. I wanted people to move fast. I wanted people to be efficient. I am already a person who doesn't have much patience, so going in with that same kind of attitude, I was in for a rude awakening. When it comes to Nigeria, honestly, you have to be ready with plan B and plan C. Something is bound to go wrong, and you have to be ready to roll with the punches. For example, our logo for Slim Girl Shapewear is hot pink. When I hired a printer to customize our store sign, I showed him photos of the logo, the store sign in Atlanta, and the fliers we had printed up for the launch so that he would be able to match the color. Everything I showed him was hot pink. Matching the color should be a no brainer, right? Wrong. This man showed up, late, of course, mere days before the launch with a *purple* sign.

Me: "Our signature color is hot pink. This sign is purple, for God's sake!"

Him: "Ah, I thought it was about the same thing."

I just knew I was being tested. I had already paid this man an 80 percent deposit to get the sign done in time for the launch, and he brought me this massive sign in the wrong color. Can you imagine? I've learned now that in Nigeria there are certain things that you need to accept up front. First and foremost is that there are going to be curveballs. If it's not the right shade you wanted, you roll with it. It was such a headache that things were not exactly the way I wanted them to be, but I had worked too hard to let this stand in my way. I was used to doing business in the States, but I was in Nigeria now, and I was learning to take deep breaths and turn lemons into lemonade.

I had hired some family members to help me manage the day-to-day operations, as well as a few sales reps I had found through a local agency. We were fully staffed, and the store was filled with our products. Now came our grand opening. Since the launch of the store in Atlanta had been such a success, I basically followed the same marketing approach in Lagos. I hired a publicist to help me create a buzz, and together we launched a big marketing campaign. We promoted on social media, placed ads in magazines, and I went to two or three radio stations to talk about our brand and promote the launch of the store. We even drove all over the city handing out fliers door-to-door. For the launch in Atlanta, we had hired a celebrity guest, and all her fans showed up for the event. I wanted to create the same kind of buzz and excitement in Lagos, so we reached out to a lot of Nigerian celebrities. Once they found out it was an American company, they upped their prices, of course. I was getting nervous, but at the last minute, we landed Nigeria's It girl, Toke Makinwa. She is basically Nigeria's Kim Kardashian. I had been working night and day for a month, and now things were finally falling into place—or close enough.

The beautiful day of our grand opening came…and only *two* customers showed up the entire day. It was so embarrassing. I had hired the best of the best in terms of Nigerian influencers, and only two people showed up? I remember feeling like I wanted the ground to open up and swallow me.

Luckily, I have a big family, and they had come out in full force to support the launch. At the time, I was discouraged, but now I've learned how things work and why the launch itself was a fail. First, I was new and no one had ever heard of me, and I could not have chosen a worse day or time. As much as people may have wanted my product, Lagos is a city where traffic rules the day, and I had foolishly booked the launch at the peak hour of weekend traffic between Lagos Island and the mainland.

The launch was a disappointment, but I was by no means defeated. I had faith in our brand and in the market. I had trained my staff according to my standards, put a family member in charge of running the store, and went back to Atlanta with such a sense of accomplishment. I was prouder of myself for opening that first store Nigeria than any of the things that I had accomplished up to then. And I had done it all myself: from the design, to the location, to setting up internet service. We opened the store officially the Monday after the launch, and in the days and weeks that followed, people started to come in droves: top celebrities, politicians' wives, everyone who was anyone. This was around the same time that we were in talks with Khloé Kardashian, so we were able to capitalize on the momentum of her post through our social media on both continents. My store became the place to go for shapewear in Lagos.

I believed strongly in the physical store, and I was relieved that we were gaining traction in the marketplace, but it was never just about making a profit or the success of one location. It was about building my business back home. The launch of the Lekki store was just one part of my larger dream. Now I was ready to make Slim Girl Shapewear a success throughout all of Nigeria.

CHAPTER 11

NO PLACE LIKE NAIJA

I wasn't the only Nigerian determined to find success back home. I was part of a wave of Nigerians returning to our motherland, seeking fortune and opportunity. Anywhere you go in the world, you will find Nigerians working in every field, from medicine to media. Having paved their way in the U.S., Britain, and everywhere else, this global diaspora of expats and Nigerian children born abroad are now returning home to invest in and revitalize the country. This brain-gain of Nigerian "repats" has enhanced the lives of all Nigerians by sparking an economic boom in every sector, from the arts, fashion, and music to technology, engineering, and business. As a business owner, it was so inspiring to be able use my own success to plant seeds back home that would be an investment in my brand and in the future of the Nigerian economy.

Three months after we launched the store on Lagos Island, I opened a second location on the mainland. The

Slimgirl.ng website was up and running, but it would take time to build the online business. At the time, ecommerce was still new to Nigeria. Consumers were not as comfortable shopping online as they are in the U.S., so in order to widen our reach, the logical move was to open a second store. Every successful entrepreneur in Nigeria has a store on Lagos Island and a store on Lagos mainland. All the celebrities and affluent Lagosians live in the Lekki area. If you're selling a luxury product, of course you want to have a store on the island because you want the rich folks to buy from you. But we also wanted to get our products into the hands of every Lagosian, so we needed to have a presence on the mainland as well. In those early days, when online shopping was still so new to Nigeria, having multiple locations definitely helped our brand. No matter where they lived in the city, people were able to come into our stores to see our products for themselves without feeling like they were taking the risk of buying from us online.

That year, I went to Nigeria six times in ten months. I would go for two or three weeks at a time, never staying away for more than a month. I needed to be in Lagos to train the staff to my standard of work. It was critical that I teach them personally how to talk to customers, how to process orders, how to log into the computers and operate a POS machine, where and how to display merchandise in the store. It was a lot to take on, but it was the only way to ensure things were being executed properly. For a full year, I was going back every other month, trying to jam everything that needed to be done into a couple of weeks and then rushing back to Atlanta to take care of my family and the business there. When I was back in the States, I'd feel like I couldn't relax. I'd be up at two o'clock in the morning checking in on the stores, then something would come up that needed my attention and I would feel like I needed to go back.

To be honest, the first year was hell. Although it was basically curveball after curveball, it never crossed my mind to give up. The harder things got, the tougher I became. The more frustrated I became, the more determined I got. I felt like I just needed to pull myself up by my bootstraps and do what needed to be done. There were so many issues, but I met every challenge head-on and tackled them all one at a time. For example, I learned to strategize my day around the ebb and flow of traffic between the mainland and the island so I wouldn't waste precious time sitting in gridlock.

Running the kind of business I wanted to run, which in the U.S. would have been easily affordable, was outrageously expensive in Nigeria. There were so many expenses I hadn't anticipated going in. I'm talking constant monthly expenses, not just initial costs. Stable electricity is a huge a problem in Nigeria. Due to corruption, you cannot rely on government-supplied electricity. Daily power outages are an inescapable part of life. A lot of shopping centers and commercial locations will say they offer a twenty-four-hour power supply to attract business owners and add a service charge to the annual rent. I don't care how upscale the location, the reality is in some places, this twenty-four-hour power supply is actually from 10:00 a.m. to 6:00 p.m. Basically you are paying a premium to enjoy twenty-four-hour electricity that is available for only eight hours a day. I discovered that I had to have a backup generator at each of our locations. And, because of the ongoing scarcity of fuel throughout the country, our biggest expense is purchasing fuel to power those generators. While the irony of fuel scarcity in an oil-rich country is not lost on anyone, we are so used to this nonsense we don't even get angry. We just roll our eyes and move on. That's the learning curve. That's Nigeria.

I had also gone back to Nigeria with the mindset of helping out my family. For years, I had prayed and hoped I would be able to bring my mom to Atlanta one day so she could have the chance to enjoy what I had worked so hard for all these years.

In my effort to give back to my family, I had also hired some of my relatives to help me manage the stores and to be my eyes and ears on the ground while I was back Atlanta. Unfortunately, this turned out to be a big mistake. For all my employees, I have deadlines, scorecards, and appraisals to evaluate and manage their performance. The problem with hiring family is that even if you have those checks and balances in place, the line between business and personal is easily blurred. I treat my staff well, but I have high expectations and exacting standards. If you work for me, I expect you to turn up on time, keep your emotions in check, and represent the brand as I would. With family, I had the same expectations as I did for the rest my staff, and that blew up in my face because they expected to be treated differently.

At the time, I was in talks with a large department store chain in Nigeria that was interested in carrying our Cinch Leggings and our Slim Gel. We were given a meeting with the head of the company, but I wasn't able to attend because I was already booked to speak at an event elsewhere in the city. I made the mistake of sending a family member to the meeting as my representative. There was some retail terminology I was well familiar with that the family member was not, and the miscommunication killed the meeting and the whole deal fell apart. Despite his best effort, it was my fault for not being there since I was the best representative for that meeting. I am black and white when it comes to business. No one is exempt, not even me or my husband. I could not continue to allow everything I had been working so hard to achieve to be put at risk. Thus, I had learned another valuable lesson: Never do business with family.

For months, my publicist had been telling me, "Juliana, you need at least one person in Lagos that can represent you while you're not here. Hire a professional and pay them good money so you can sleep at night." Thankfully, I already had a woman on staff I felt was capable of stepping into the position of managing the stores for me. I decided to pay her more than she earned at her last job, which was more than I paid my other employees. It seemed extravagant, but it was the best option. In fact, when I calculated how much I was spending on travel, hotels, and airfare every few weeks, I realized that in the long run I'd be saving money if I had someone I could truly rely on to run things in Lagos.

It took a while for me able to take a step back. For the first year and a half, I handled every little detail of the day-to-day operations of the stores and the website, even down to paying the phone and utility bills. When I got pregnant with our second son, Eze, I could no longer be rushing back and forth between Atlanta and Lagos. I worked right up until the day he was born, but it stretched me thin. I realized it was time for me to loosen the reigns. Thankfully, this woman proved to me she could handle the responsibility. I was even able to put her in charge of the launch of our third store in the capital, Abuja. I put a lot of checks and balances in place. The surveillance cameras are linked to my phone and my computer. I do video conferencing with the staff. Anything that's ordered in the stores goes through me. Our entire operation is streamlined and integrated, enabling me to run the business from Atlanta. The truth is, since I promoted her, I have not had to go to Nigeria for two years. That's how well things are being run. That's how beneficial hiring her has been. I can sleep at night knowing my Nigerian baby is in capable hands.

She is still with me to this day. She takes pride in her work and gives me 110 percent every single day. I refer to her as my personal assistant in situations where I need her to send an email or attend a meeting on my behalf, but in practical terms, she is my operations manager in Nigeria. She does everything from contacting agencies for ads to handling customer service reps and inventory. She does all the hiring and firing and makes sure everything is run properly. I still control all money that goes in and out, from payroll to processing orders. That is one responsibility I will never delegate. I remember reading somewhere that Oprah Winfrey said the one thing she still does all the time is sign all her checks. That always stuck with me. No matter how big you get, no matter how busy you are, you need to know every nickel and dime that goes out the door.

Now that I wasn't splitting my time between two continents, I was able to focus my attention and correct some of the mistakes I had made early on in my haste to establish a foothold in the Nigerian market. Going in, I had approached each store with a minimalist strategy. It was always a small shop in an upscale neighborhood. We did our best to manage storage, but with the growth of the website, it got to the point where we had so much inventory we needed more space to house it all. We also needed a dedicated base of operations for the online business. We opened a warehouse with an office and a showroom on the mainland. Because I was pregnant at the time, Mansour flew to Nigeria to oversee things.

That year we also changed locations for the two stores in Lagos. Tired of paying way too much for the space on Lagos Island, I found another location in the Lekki area that was bigger, had more exposure, and was in a better building, for half the rent we had been paying. I was also unhappy with the location of the store on the mainland. I had chosen a busy neighborhood, but I didn't pay close enough attention to the look of the environment or consider how this could impact my brand integrity. Since the landlord did not maintain or clean the building, even though the store itself was upscale and polished, the environment wasn't appealing. With the warehouse nearby, I could save money on rent and resolve our location issue by moving the store into our showroom. Because it wasn't far from the previous location, thankfully customers didn't mind detouring and coming to the new space.

One of the things I'm most proud of is how we were able to build the online business in Nigeria. In the early days, sales at the stores were way higher than through the website. Within three years, it has grown to about fifty-fifty, and believe me, it was a long, hard climb to get there. For all the challenges we faced when it came to making the physical stores a success, nothing can compare to what we had to go through to get customers to trust buying from us online. The first hurdle was just being able to ship our products anywhere in the country. The more reach I have, the more sales I can make, so I thought my prayers were answered when I found a logistics company that shipped to every remote location in Nigeria. That was a huge win for us, but the real challenge turned out to be much more complicated than logistics. In order for the website to thrive and survive, we had to overcome Nigerians' distrust of the concept of prepay. Due to bad trade experiences in the past, some Nigerians do not feel comfortable prepaying for goods online from an unfamiliar source. Online businesses have no choice but to rely on a pay-on-delivery system, which causes nothing but headaches.

With pay-on-delivery, we learned quickly never to assume the customer really does want what they've ordered. You can't just process an order and ship it. You literally have to call and confirm every single order because the customer checks out without paying. If they change their minds or miss the delivery window, you have no choice but to eat the cost of the shipping. Even then, it's no guarantee. I can't tell you how many times we'd call the customer to confirm, only for the driver to travel six hundred miles to some remote location and the person wasn't home to receive their shipment. Or the driver would get there and the customer would try on the items and then decide they didn't want them anymore. We're talking about intimate apparel, mind you, preventing the items from being restocked. Having paid for that delivery, I'd be out of pocket for the items *and* the shipping. If a customer decided they only wanted one of the items they had ordered, the driver was not familiar with our pricing, so they could basically just pay whatever they wanted and send him on his way. I had even heard stories from other Nigerian business owners of disgruntled former employees placing a big order online only for that company to attempt delivery and have the entire order rejected. We went through this nonsense for almost two years. Thankfully, I had my husband's support, and we went through it together because it was such a crazy, mind-bending experience. I was practically losing my mind with frustration.

I tried implementing a policy of not allowing customers to open the package until they had paid for their items, but that totally backfired on me. Our customers did not like this at all. *What? I can't see the product? Then I don't want it.* It actually ended up increasing order rejections. I was so frustrated that I started to second-guess everything. Then I came up with a brilliant idea. I told my staff, "This is what we're going to do. We will still charge for shipping for all our pay-on-delivery orders, but we're going to offer *free* shipping if customers prepay." Once we started advertising that we offered the option of free delivery all over the country, which is rare in Nigeria, our prepay orders soared, and we stopped having all those issues with delivery. You'd be surprised how the incentive of saving an extra five or ten dollars can influence the consumer.

My next big idea was to stop outsourcing our delivery logistics within Lagos. We bought a motorbike, with a compartment on the back for packages, and hired a dispatch driver. Having our own logistics in Lagos allowed us to offer express shipping within the city. We got our products to our customers faster, and we got paid faster. Now when we charge a customer who wants pay-on-delivery, that money comes directly into our pocket. I made sure the bike was customized in our signature hot pink with our logo emblazoned on the side. We even have the driver wear a hot pink helmet. It's been great for brand-recognition. To this day, people all over Lagos know us as the "pink bike company."

Finding ways to scale the business presented new challenges, but I was on a roll. I found ways to cut costs and cheaper ways to market. I understood the Nigerian economy;

not everyone has as much disposable income as they do in the U.S. I wanted Nigerians to be able to try my product, because a happy customer will come back to shop again. I wanted brand recognition, so I had to figure out how to get a product that the average Nigerian consumer can afford without compromising quality. I used to spend a fortune on shipping to Nigeria. Wanting total oversight, all the inventory from our manufacturers came through our warehouse in Atlanta first, and then we shipped to Nigeria. Eventually, I got smarter and streamlined the process. Now we ship directly from our manufacturers to Nigeria. By removing myself from the equation, we were able to save money without compromising quality.

In the early days, I was whirlwind mess, but I was determined to make it work. Whenever we encountered a roadblock, I found a solution. My perseverance paid off, because we have finally started to find much stronger footing. One of my proudest moments for Slim Girl Nigeria was when my sister told me about a customer who had called to order a pair of our Cinch Leggings. She was getting the woman's information and processing her order over the phone when she recognized the name and realized it was one of our neighbors we had known since we were kids. She didn't even know Slim Girl was my company, but she had seen the Khloé post and was intrigued by our brand. I felt such a sense of excitement and accomplishment when I heard this. Our reach had finally extended so far it had actually come full circle. It felt like we had finally made it in Nigeria. It was the same feeling I had when the cincher lady passed by our store in Atlanta to spy on us.

After three years, we are finally making some profit, but the truth was, if we had to live on our profits in Nigeria alone, we would never have survived. For the first two years, we ran at a loss. But Juliana did not care. I had this sentimental feeling about running my businesses in Nigeria. My drive came from a determination to conquer my homecoming. Sometimes it's about more than just making money. You have to persevere when it means something so deeply personal to you. I believe in the future of the economy, not just as a Nigerian, but also as a businesswoman. Nigeria is exciting, but you have to be able to stay the course and come up with elegant solutions to the quirks of the culture. You can't fight against or change the mentality, but you can figure out ways to make it work for you. That is the key to success in the global market: understanding the mindset of your consumer and making it work for your business. The trick is to be able to tailor your business philosophy to the needs of the market, as well as bend that market to fit your model. It's a balancing act.

Nigeria is not an easy place to do business, especially for an American. The triumph of being able to navigate my way through every challenge was a reward in itself. Even if I have been Americanized, I'm still Nigerian. It is my Naija-ness, that quintessential Nigerian spirit, that drives me in all things I do. We Nigerians are survivors. We are proud of our culture and our identity. We are industrious, hard-working, ingenious, and resilient. Let's face it, we need to be all those things, because Nigeria can be extremely frustrating and inefficient. Yet it is also a country of incredible beauty, a land of limitless opportunity where anything and everything is possible.

CHAPTER 12

FAMILY JULES

A s my business began to blossom and grow on both continents, I could have been content with the success we had already achieved. I could have been satisfied with conquering the shapewear market. I could have... but I wasn't. As you have probably figured out by now, I thrive on challenges. I wanted more. I wanted to build a global brand that went far beyond a single product category. When I envisioned the future of my company, I saw us expanding into swimwear, lingerie, beauty products, accessories, and beyond. I wanted our customers to say to themselves, "I need lip gloss," or "I'm looking for a cute bikini," and automatically think of us. In order to do this, I was faced with two simultaneous challenges. The first was to rebrand our image as a company that sold more than cinchers and shapewear, and the second was to determine which products our customers wanted most.

In our quest to fine-tune our position in the marketplace, Mansour and I kept coming back to the idea that if we were to expand our brand, we needed a name for the company that spoke to a wider market. We wanted to branch into different kinds of apparel and beauty products, but we were locked into the cincher name for our website. If I could do it all again, I would choose a name that had room for expansion from the outset. I've learned now that brands evolve, so your name needs to be able to grow with your company. We had started out as 1800Cinchers.com. As we expanded into the larger shapewear market, we started using Slim Girl Shapewear, which became the name for our Instagram page and the store in Atlanta. As we established our brand in the Nigerian market, we used Slim Girl Shapewear there as well. We had been 1800Cinchers in the U.S. through all the big publicity: *The Wendy Williams Show*, the Khloé Kardashian post, and in all the magazine features. As reluctant as I was to lose that brand recognition, the fact was we were no longer a cincher company, or even a shapewear company. The goal was to become a brand that women could turn to for *all* their beauty needs. The challenge was to find a name that was broad enough for us to expand but which also captured the essence of who we were.

It took my husband and me about a year and a half to commit to the idea of change and to come up with the right name. It had to be something that reflected our identity and celebrated feminine beauty. My own beauty philosophy has always been about the confidence you get from looking fabulous. I wanted to provide my customers with a range of products that make everyday women look and feel beautiful. I am very tuned in to the changing ways that women see their bodies. Having a positive body image is so important to our customers, and my mission has always been to provide them with the tools they need to look fabulous, ensuring they feel good about their bodies. With that mission in mind, in 2016, 1800Cinchers was reborn as BodyFab. The name says it all.

I was so excited about rebranding and all the possibilities it opened up for us, yet at the same time it also presented us with new challenges. Initially, we lost some customers who just didn't feel comfortable buying from BodyFab because they didn't trust we were the same company. Even though 1800Cinchers.com takes you directly to the BodyFab website, we still got calls from confused customers. We would have to read our returning customers their order history to reassure them that we were the same company. Although it wasn't easy, with diligent attention to customer service, we won back our loyal customer base, and they began to trust that they would be getting the same quality products as always.

When we saw what was happening with BodyFab and 1800Cinchers in the U.S., we made the decision not to change our name in Nigeria. I had watched my mother's pure water business struggle after she lost the name of her company. She had spent years building her business and cultivating a loyal consumer base, but when she had to change her name, she lost brand recognition and her customers took their business elsewhere. The business hung on for a few more years, but it never fully recovered. While it's an age-old issue with marketing, in Nigeria it's even harder to win back customer loyalty than it is in the U.S. I had invested so much time, money, and energy into marketing the Slim Girl brand and into building web integrity for the online business that we decided not to rebrand in Nigeria. We would focus BodyFab on the U.S. market and remain Slim Girl in Nigeria.

We had been gradually introducing new products in both markets, testing the waters to see what worked and what didn't. The more products you have, the more revenue you are able to make. It's that simple. It's good to start expansion within the same genre, but if your brand is strong enough, ultimately you can branch into entirely different markets. It's basically the same model as Amazon: the more options and variety you're able to provide, the more likely customers are to buy from you, and the more money you can make. That is honestly and clearly the reasoning behind our rebranding and expansion. If you have a limited product line, you are limiting the customers that can buy from you.

When it came time to decide what our next product lines would be, as always, I looked to our customers for direction. It all starts from the buzz we get from customer feedback. If customers start asking for tableware, you will definitely see me selling BodyFab tableware. Since we were already selling apparel that fell into the category of intimate wear, we had a lot of customers reaching out to us about lingerie, bras, and swimwear. As we began to branch into these new products, I had absorbed the lessons of our past experiences. No amount of market research can truly predict consumer appetite for a particular product. Instead of us diving in head-on and investing in products we didn't know for sure our customers would buy, we started importing items we knew our manufacturers already sold successfully in small quantities, just to see how our customers would react. This reduced costs and minimized risk.

The swimsuits were a huge hit in the U.S. We cater to moms who prefer not to show their bellies, but they still want to look hot and sexy. We carried swimsuits in sizes up to 6XL, and our customers loved them because they were high-waisted bikinis that provided a lot of coverage but were also stylish. In fact, we have had so much success with the swim-suits in the U.S. that we are now working on designs for our own line of swimwear for women. With lingerie and bras, we were less successful in the U.S. Interestingly, it was the exact reverse in Nigeria; lingerie and bras were huge, but swimsuits didn't pick up much at all. By taking my time, I was able to learn the appetites of our different markets and cater individually to each without tying up too much capital in inventory that wasn't going to sell.

Designing our own swimwear is such an exciting new venture for us, but there has definitely been a learning curve. We sketch designs, select fabrics and materials, and send it to our manufacturers. They send back a prototype for us to test out and determine if the structure of the design is realistic. When you are working on apparel for women, it has to have the right coverage and fit. With waist cinchers, sizing is straightforward, but with swimsuits, sizing can get very complicated, especially if there are two pieces. You can wear a size L for the bottom piece but an XXL on top. It's a much more complex piece of apparel in terms of fit, so you have to have different variations, and it can be frustrating and costly to produce and sell. We try and make sure that the design works from a technical standpoint, but that it also makes sense when you put it on. As always, I have samples made in my size so I can test the design out on myself before I unleash them on my customers.

After we went through the BodyFab rebrand, we decided to streamline our whole operation in the U.S. We closed down the warehouse and found a fulfillment center in Atlanta to process, package, and ship all of our orders. They handle the returns and exchanges and house our inventory. Outsourcing to a fulfillment center freed us of all the overhead that came with having the warehouse. There's a lot of liability when you have employees that you're responsible for. You have to consider liability insurance, workers' comp, medical benefits for full-time employees, dealing with temps for workers who call in sick or have an emergency; all those extra office issues that come up here and there. And then, of course, all the expenses that come with having people in the building using up energy: cable, internet, phone, electricity, heat. It was just too much to manage for a mother of two little boys. On top of that, dealing with Nigeria took a lot of my energy. Nigeria was not a small, one-time project; it was a full-time energy-draining experience. It was a no brainer when we found a fulfillment company that handled all these things for us. We were able to operate just as efficiently, but with less cost and less energy.

We went through the same streamlining process with our customer service. With 1800Cinchers, we initially outsourced customer service. When we opened the warehouse, we decided to house customer service, and now we have outsourced again. We found a better-qualified team of representatives to handle customer needs with precision and care, which again means less overhead and less liability. We also have a team of freelancers we pay on a monthly retainer: graphic designers who make banners and create all our logos and graphics; a web designer who helps us make tweaks here and there on the website; and, of course, our PR team that handles marketing and outreach. We are a much leaner and more efficient operation, which means Mansour and I are not tied down with having to handle all the day-to-day details. Now we have the space to focus on expanding our product lines and building a better brand.

One of the most exciting things that came out of outsourcing our order fulfillment and customer service was that I was able pursue one of my passions. Anyone who knows me knows I am a total reality television addict. I binge-watch shows like *Growing Up Hip-Hop*, *Jersey Shore*, *Love & Hip-Hop*, and the whole *Real Housewives* franchise. I love a good train wreck. One of the perks of marketing a global brand is that I have access to these celebrities because we do advertising with them. I decided to try my hand at a web chat show. We called it *Jules Uncut*, to give it that intimate, uncensored feel. We did eight episodes and interviewed celebrities like Kenya Moore, "Tiny" Harris, Kandi Burruss, Brandon Barnes, Angie Stone, and Musiq Soulchild. We did a really fun segment where I would come up with Nigerian names and tribes for our guests and taught them how to say different phrases in Broken English. Nigerians loved it, and we found ourselves in talks with a Nigerian television network to pick up the show for the second season.

The whole experience of *Jules Uncut* was such a high for me. I loved the glamour and the excitement of being out front as a personality. However, when we began the process of taking the show to the next level, I had to make some difficult choices about the direction I wanted my life and my business to go. It was one thing when we were filming in Atlanta, but if the show was to grow and actually become a money-making venture, I would have to travel for interviews and devote myself to the project completely. Creating a show takes so much out of you, from booking celebrities and prepping for the interviews, to editing the footage into an episode, to dealing with hair, wardrobe, and makeup. It never ends. *Jules Uncut* was a hobby, and I enjoyed doing it, but it was time to get back to reality. I needed to focus on what mattered the most to me, and the show wasn't where I wanted to direct all my energy.

As much as it was fun to interview all those celebrities, I didn't have the same passion for it that I do for business. I didn't want to live the celebrity life. It was an amazing opportunity, but I could not run my company the way I wanted *and* have the show if I wanted to be present for my family. As an entrepreneur who's also a mother, it was just way too much to take on. The point of us having our own company is to do what we really love. And while I did love the excitement that the show had brought to my life, my family and the business have to come first.

I have so much drive and ambition that I can easily find myself in over my head, but I always catch myself when I find I have bitten off more than I can chew. I'm not one to suffer through. When things become too much for me, I pause and reroute myself. I am confident enough in myself and my choices that I have no regrets walking away from something that is not right for me, regardless of what anyone else thinks or expects of me. Motherhood has changed me. I am focused on what matters the most, raising my children and running my business. Everything else is secondary. That's how I live now.

When I finally took a step back, I found such joy in the simplicity and peacefulness of it. Mansour and I were so overwhelmed for so many years. When we went through the Wendy frenzy, we were so busy that we had no time to relax. Then I kept putting more and more pressure on growing the business in Nigeria. When I gave birth to my younger son, I realized I couldn't always be burning the candle on both ends anymore. My sons need my time and attention, especially Eze; he's a bundle of energy and wants to play all the time. I am focused now on what truly matters. It's about finding that work/life balance. What was all this for if I don't take the time to enjoy my beautiful children? Mansour and I are still running the business the way we want to run it, but it's not taking over my life the way it was before. We are still all about building that million-dollar side hustle, but we're also about taking the time to enjoy our success.

I've gotten so much better at balancing work and family. Honestly, it's still a struggle, but I've learned how to cut back. The biggest challenge was just being able to step aside and allow my staff to do their jobs. I have a whole team in Nigeria, and for the longest time I would never let them handle the day-to-day details of running the company. It took me a while, but after a while, I learned to let them manage themselves and to handle things like inventory and marketing. I still micromanage, but I'm way more relaxed than I was before. For the first two years, I was literally supervising every aspect of the business in Nigeria because I needed my team to understand how serious I was about how I wanted the business run. I've trained them well enough now that it is time for me to let go. The operation runs so smoothly now that I could go a whole week without having to check up on them. Well, to be honest, I still do still check up on them every day, but baby steps!

Going global has not been easy. It took years of grueling twelve-hour flights, traveling back and forth between two continents, painstaking attention to details, countless sleepless nights, and untold sweat, pain, and frustration. We have made mistakes in Nigeria, but along the way we learned what it takes to bring e-commerce to a country where it is still at a very early stage. We continue to learn and grow every single day.

I never sleep more than three or four hours at a stretch. That's an important thing for any aspiring entrepreneur or small business owner to grasp. Especially in the early days of building your business, getting eight hours of sleep is not going to happen. I experience burnout a lot. There are times I'm so exhausted I can't think straight or be creative. My day starts a 9:00 a.m., I'm communicating with the Nigerian team, working on marketing strategies, keeping up on admin work, accounting, and making sure official documents are filled out properly. I'm overseeing orders that have come through, trying to sort out brand ambassadors, looking through customer complaints and requests. I'm overseeing the operations of the business and filling in gaps. What are we promoting today? What celebrities have we reached out to for social media promotions?

At around 7:00 p.m. is when I start sourcing. I'm communicating with our manufacturers in China, Colombia, and India, placing orders and negotiating prices. At around 10:00 p.m., I usually pass out from sheer exhaustion. Then I'm up again at 2:00 a.m. to check up on Nigeria, where the workday is just about to begin. I'll turn on the surveillance cameras to check they've opened the stores. Are they clocking in? Have they cleaned up? What are they doing? At around 3:00 a.m., my son Eze usually wakes up crying for food, so I'm stopped in my tracks. My husband wakes up too, and for the next two or three hours, we're dealing with the baby while still trying to manage Nigeria. At around 5:00 a.m., I go back to sleep and get a couple of hours in before starting up at 9:00 a.m. to begin the whole process all over again.

I'm operating in multiple time zones all day long, but I wouldn't have it any other way. My husband likes to joke that my hobby is work. No matter where we are or what we're doing, I'm always on my laptop or my phone researching and reading up on market trends. There's a part of my brain that is always focused on work because I have maintained my side hustle mentality. I'm not trying to turn into a big corporate machine. I don't have board members or branding experts who would give me their expertise. Mansour and I have to be the experts. We have to be creative and stay on top of global markets. And then we still do the regular mom and dad things. We drop the boys off and pick them up from school and day care. We take them to the doctor for check-ups and shots. We are there for meals and play time. It's a constant balancing act.

Whatever it is that you are doing, you have to be obsessed. You can't give up. If you are obsessed with what you're doing, you will work hard and put in the hours it takes to build something from nothing. It won't feel like work because every minute you are thinking and breathing and eating what you love. Ideas come to you in the middle of the night, and you wake up and write them down because you don't want that inspiration to slip away. That is the side hustle mentality.

You also need to have a deep-rooted sense of self-confidence. If you don't have it naturally, get it somewhere. Find it. Build it. My story is about what you can achieve with hard work and a healthy dose of confidence. I came from a third world country with no plan and no money, but I turned my side hustle into a thriving global brand. Start small and work your way up. It doesn't have to be e-commerce; it can be anything that you have the passion and drive to commit yourself to body, mind, and soul. It's never too late. Don't be afraid of failure.

During this business journey, I have been a daughter, a sister, a wife, and a mother. I am often been viewed as a role model for immigrants, entrepreneurs, women, and minorities, a role I do not take lightly. These are heavy and blessed responsibilities that require time, one of the scarcest resources you have when you are building a company. My hope is that you will walk away from this book with a true understanding of what it takes to be an entrepreneur—the tears, the laughter, the panic, the loneliness, and the self-doubt. It goes far beyond the brain and deep into the heart. Building a million-dollar side hustle is an epic journey, but as you travel that long and windy road, you will encounter moments of pure joy and triumph that come from succeeding at something you love.

While shaping your destiny is not easy, it is rewarding beyond your wildest dreams.

ABOUT THE AUTHOR

Juliana Richards is the founder and CEO of Slim Girl Shapewear, a major worldwide player with physical stores on three continents and a strong online retail presence. Her leading clothing line is shapewear, undergarments that slim the waist and smooth and control one's figure. She also has introduced a line of lingerie with the intention of leveraging her well-respected brand to gain market share in this thirty-two-billion-dollar global industry.

Born and raised in Nigeria, she moved to America as a teenager by herself to pursue her dream of becoming a lawyer. She started her company while in college studying accounting. In less than ten years, this entrepreneur, wife, and mother turned Slim Girl Shapewear into what is considered one of the world's most lucrative lines of women's wear.

Slim Girl Shapewear has been featured on *The Real* and *The Wendy Williams Show* and in publications such as *Rolling Out, Examiner, Atlanta Black Star, OK! Magazine, Health Magazine, New York Magazine, Vegan Life,* and *Body Magazine.*